The iMac™ FOR DUMMIES®
QUICK REFERENCE

by Jennifer Watson

IDG BOOKS WORLDWIDE

IDG Books Worldwide, Inc.
An International Data Group Company

Foster City, CA ✦ Chicago, IL ✦ Indianapolis, IN ✦ New York, NY

The iMac™ For Dummies® Quick Reference

Published by
IDG Books Worldwide, Inc.
An International Data Group Company
919 E. Hillsdale Blvd.
Suite 400
Foster City, CA 94404
www.idgbooks.com (IDG Books Worldwide Web site)
www.dummies.com (Dummies Press Web site)

Library of Congress Catalog Card No.: 00-01843

ISBN: 0-7645-0718-4

Printed in the United States of America

10 9 8 7 6 5 4 3 2 1

1P/QR/QV/QQ/IN

Distributed in the United States by IDG Books Worldwide, Inc.

Distributed by CDG Books Canada Inc. for Canada; by Transworld Publishers Limited in the United Kingdom; by IDG Norge Books for Norway; by IDG Sweden Books for Sweden; by IDG Books Australia Publishing Corporation Pty. Ltd. for Australia and New Zealand; by TransQuest Publishers Pte Ltd. for Singapore, Malaysia, Thailand, Indonesia, and Hong Kong; by Gotop Information Inc. for Taiwan; by ICG Muse, Inc. for Japan; by Intersoft for South Africa; by Eyrolles for France; by International Thomson Publishing for Germany, Austria and Switzerland; by Distribuidora Cuspide for Argentina; by LR International for Brazil; by Galileo Libros for Chile; by Ediciones ZETA S.C.R. Ltda. for Peru; by WS Computer Publishing Corporation, Inc., for the Philippines; by Contemporanea de Ediciones for Venezuela; by Express Computer Distributors for the Caribbean and West Indies; by Micronesia Media Distributor, Inc. for Micronesia; by Chips Computadoras S.A. de C.V. for Mexico; by Editorial Norma de Panama S.A. for Panama; by American Bookshops for Finland.

For general information on IDG Books Worldwide's books in the U.S., please call our Consumer Customer Service department at 800-762-2974. For reseller information, including discounts and premium sales, please call our Reseller Customer Service department at 800-434-3422.

For information on where to purchase IDG Books Worldwide's books outside the U.S., please contact our International Sales department at 317-596-5530 or fax 317-572-4002.

For consumer information on foreign language translations, please contact our Customer Service department at 1-800-434-3422, fax 317-572-4002, or e-mail rights@idgbooks.com.

For information on licensing foreign or domestic rights, please phone +1-650-653-7098.

For sales inquiries and special prices for bulk quantities, please contact our Order Services department at 800-434-3422 or write to the address above.

For information on using IDG Books Worldwide's books in the classroom or for ordering examination copies, please contact our Educational Sales department at 800-434-2086 or fax 317-572-4005.

For press review copies, author interviews, or other publicity information, please contact our Public Relations department at 650-653-7000 or fax 650-653-7500.

For authorization to photocopy items for corporate, personal, or educational use, please contact Copyright Clearance Center, 222 Rosewood Drive, Danvers, MA 01923, or fax 978-750-4470.

About the Author

Jennifer Watson is the author of *Teach Yourself the iMac* and a dozen other popular computer books.

ABOUT IDG BOOKS WORLDWIDE

Welcome to the world of IDG Books Worldwide.

IDG Books Worldwide, Inc., is a subsidiary of International Data Group, the world's largest publisher of computer-related information and the leading global provider of information services on information technology. IDG was founded more than 30 years ago by Patrick J. McGovern and now employs more than 9,000 people worldwide. IDG publishes more than 290 computer publications in over 75 countries. More than 90 million people read one or more IDG publications each month.

Launched in 1990, IDG Books Worldwide is today the #1 publisher of best-selling computer books in the United States. We are proud to have received eight awards from the Computer Press Association in recognition of editorial excellence and three from Computer Currents' First Annual Readers' Choice Awards. Our best-selling ...For Dummies® series has more than 50 million copies in print with translations in 31 languages. IDG Books Worldwide, through a joint venture with IDG's Hi-Tech Beijing, became the first U.S. publisher to publish a computer book in the People's Republic of China. In record time, IDG Books Worldwide has become the first choice for millions of readers around the world who want to learn how to better manage their businesses.

Our mission is simple: Every one of our books is designed to bring extra value and skill-building instructions to the reader. Our books are written by experts who understand and care about our readers. The knowledge base of our editorial staff comes from years of experience in publishing, education, and journalism — experience we use to produce books to carry us into the new millennium. In short, we care about books, so we attract the best people. We devote special attention to details such as audience, interior design, use of icons, and illustrations. And because we use an efficient process of authoring, editing, and desktop publishing our books electronically, we can spend more time ensuring superior content and less time on the technicalities of making books.

You can count on our commitment to deliver high-quality books at competitive prices on topics you want to read about. At IDG Books Worldwide, we continue in the IDG tradition of delivering quality for more than 30 years. You'll find no better book on a subject than one from IDG Books Worldwide.

John Kilcullen
Chairman and CEO
IDG Books Worldwide, Inc.

WINNER

Eighth Annual Computer Press Awards ≥1992

IX WINNER

Ninth Annual Computer Press Awards ≥1993

WINNER

X WINNER

Tenth Annual Computer Press Awards ≥1994

XI WINNER

Eleventh Annual Computer Press Awards ≥1995

IDG is the world's leading IT media, research and exposition company. Founded in 1964, IDG had 1997 revenues of $2.05 billion and has more than 9,000 employees worldwide. IDG offers the widest range of media options that reach IT buyers in 75 countries representing 95% of worldwide IT spending. IDG's diverse product and services portfolio spans six key areas including print publishing, online publishing, expositions and conferences, market research, education and training, and global marketing services. More than 90 million people read one or more of IDG's 290 magazines and newspapers, including IDG's leading global brands — Computerworld, PC World, Network World, Macworld and the Channel World family of publications. IDG Books Worldwide is one of the fastest-growing computer book publishers in the world, with more than 700 titles in 36 languages. The "...For Dummies®" series alone has more than 50 million copies in print. IDG offers online users the largest network of technology-specific Web sites around the world through IDG.net (http://www.idg.net), which comprises more than 225 targeted Web sites in 55 countries worldwide. International Data Corporation (IDC) is the world's largest provider of information technology data, analysis and consulting, with research centers in over 41 countries and more than 400 research analysts worldwide. IDG World Expo is a leading producer of more than 168 globally branded conferences and expositions in 35 countries including E3 (Electronic Entertainment Expo), Macworld Expo, ComNet, Windows World Expo, ICE (Internet Commerce Expo), Agenda, DEMO, and Spotlight. IDG's training subsidiary, ExecuTrain, is the world's largest computer training company, with more than 230 locations worldwide and 785 training courses. IDG Marketing Services helps industry-leading IT companies build international brand recognition by developing global integrated marketing programs via IDG's print, online and exposition products worldwide. Further information about the company can be found at www.idg.com.   1/26/00

Publisher's Acknowledgments

We're proud of this book; please register your comments through our IDG Books Worldwide Online Registration Form located at http://my2cents.dummies.com.

Some of the people who helped bring this book to market include the following:

Acquisitions, Editorial, and Media Development

Senior Project Editor: Pat O'Brien

Acquisitions Editor: Michael Roney

Senior Copy Editor: Ted Cains

Proof Editor: Dwight Ramsey

Technical Editor: Phil Robertson

Editorial Manager: Rev Mengle

Editorial Assistant: Candace Nicholson

Special Help: Tonya Maddox

Production

Project Coordinator: Emily Perkins

Layout and Graphics: Amy Adrian, Joe Bucki, Angela F. Hunckler, Tracy K. Oliver, Brent Savage, Janet Seib

Proofreaders: Laura Albert, Corey Bowen, Laura Bowman

Indexer: Liz Cunningham

Special Help
Amanda M. Foxworth

General and Administrative

IDG Books Worldwide, Inc.: John Kilcullen, CEO

IDG Books Technology Publishing Group: Richard Swadley, Senior Vice President and Publisher; Walter R. Bruce III, Vice President and Publisher; Joseph Wikert, Vice President and Publisher; Mary Bednarek, Vice President and Director, Product Development; Andy Cummings, Publishing Director, General User Group; Mary C. Corder, Editorial Director; Barry Pruett, Publishing Director

IDG Books Consumer Publishing Group: Roland Elgey, Senior Vice President and Publisher; Kathleen A. Welton, Vice President and Publisher; Kevin Thornton, Acquisitions Manager; Kristin A. Cocks, Editorial Director

IDG Books Internet Publishing Group: Brenda McLaughlin, Senior Vice President and Publisher; Sofia Marchant, Online Marketing Manager

IDG Books Production for Branded Press: Debbie Stailey, Director of Production; Cindy L. Phipps, Manager of Project Coordination, Production Proofreading, and Indexing; Tony Augsburger, Manager of Prepress, Reprints, and Systems; Laura Carpenter, Production Control Manager; Shelley Lea, Supervisor of Graphics and Design; Debbie J. Gates, Production Systems Specialist; Robert Springer, Supervisor of Proofreading; Kathie Schutte, Production Supervisor

Packaging and Book Design: Patty Page, Manager, Promotions Marketing

♦

The publisher would like to give special thanks to Patrick J. McGovern, without whom this book would not have been possible.

♦

Contents at a Glance

Table of Contents

The Big Picture: iMac

iMac

Ready to get your feet wet before you dive into the rest of this book? The Big Picture shows you a snapshot of your iMac and what it can do for you. If you're a beginner, use this section to acquaint yourself with your new iMac. Seasoned Mac pros can benefit from the general overview and project ideas in The Big Picture.

In this part, you find the basics on using the iMac desktop and dialog boxes, identifying the parts of the screen, and the manner in which you can use various components. This part also introduces basic tasks, such as powering up your iMac, opening applications and files, and saving your work. The last section of this part details several projects you can do on your iMac, such as watching and making movies.

In this part . . .

- ✔ **What you see**
- ✔ **The Control Strip Table**
- ✔ **The basics**
- ✔ **What you can do**

What You See: The iMac Desktop

The figure shows a typical iMac desktop — your home base. Important components of the desktop are pointed out for your reference. For more information on these components and their functions, explore the sections cited below.

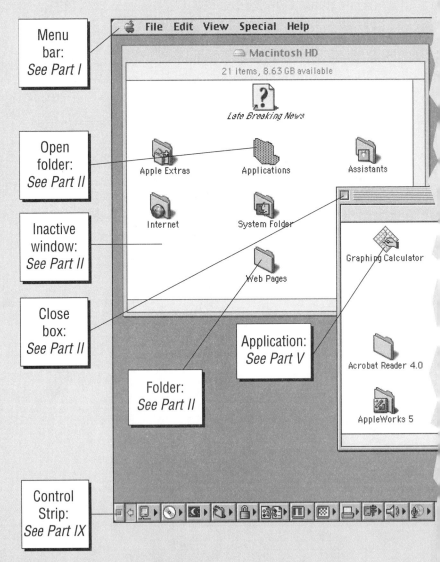

Menu bar:
See Part I

Open folder:
See Part II

Inactive window:
See Part II

Close box:
See Part II

Control Strip:
See Part IX

Application:
See Part V

Folder:
See Part II

File   Edit   View   Special   Help

Macintosh HD

21 items, 8.63 GB available

Late Breaking News

Apple Extras   Applications   Assistants

Internet   System Folder

Web Pages

Graphing Calculator

Acrobat Reader 4.0

AppleWorks 5

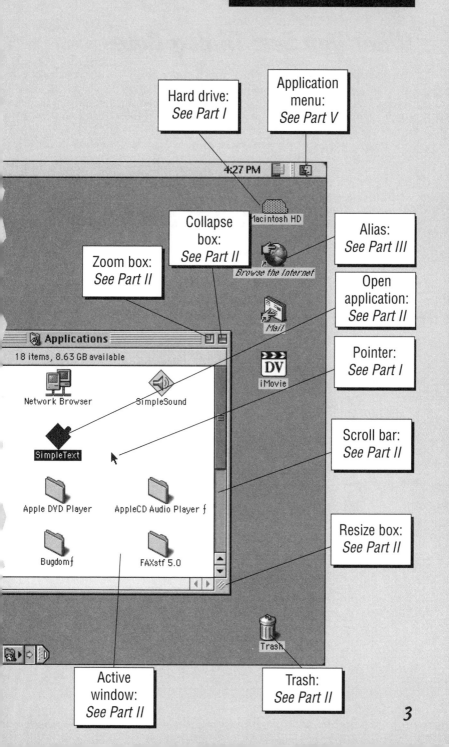

Hard drive:
See Part I

Application menu:
See Part V

Collapse box:
See Part II

Zoom box:
See Part II

Alias:
See Part III

Open application:
See Part II

Pointer:
See Part I

Scroll bar:
See Part II

Resize box:
See Part II

Active window:
See Part II

Trash:
See Part II

4:27 PM

Macintosh HD

Browse the Internet

Mail

DV
iMovie

Applications

18 items, 8.63 GB available

Network Browser

SimpleSound

SimpleText

Apple DVD Player

AppleCD Audio Player ƒ

Bugdom ƒ

FAXstf 5.0

Trash

3

What You See: Dialog Boxes

You and your iMac communicate through *dialog boxes* — your iMac asks you questions in dialog boxes, and you provide information through them in return. Dialog boxes can appear on-screen throughout your iMac: on the desktop, in applications, and in Control Panels. A dialog box window appears in front of everything that may already be on your screen, and you must either provide the requested information or dismiss (cancel) it to make the dialog box go away.

The figure below shows a typical iMac dialog box. This particular dialog box appears when you open the AppleWorks application and choose the Format⇨Section command. This is an excellent example of a dialog box, because it contains most of the dialog box controls you are likely to encounter on your iMac.

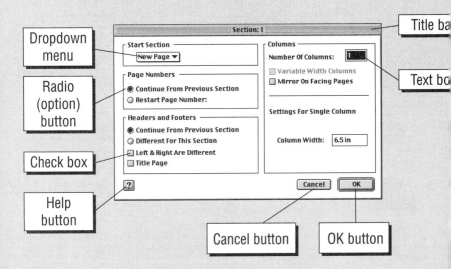

- ✔ **Button:** Clicking a dialog box button does something else.

- ✔ **Cancel button:** Click this if you change your mind. None of the changes you made to the dialog box will take effect.

- ✔ **Check box:** A square box that you can click to turn an option on or off. A check mark in the box indicates the option is turned on.

- ✔ **Drop-down menu:** A list of things you can choose from. These are actually buttons with a small arrow that points down — click the arrow to reveal the list.

- ✔ **Help button:** Click the button with a question mark symbol to display information about this dialog box.

- ✔ **List box (not shown):** Choose an item from the list, usually by single-clicking it.

- ✔ **OK button:** Click this after you make your dialog box selections and want to continue.

- ✔ **Radio (option) button:** Click one of these round buttons to enable an option. Only one radio button in a group can be enabled.

- ✔ **Spinner (not shown):** A control with two arrows (one points up and one points down) that changes a number in a text box. Click one of the arrows to increase or decrease the number displayed in the text box.

- ✔ **Tab (not shown):** Click a tab along the top of the dialog box to display a new set of controls or options.

- ✔ **Text box:** Type a desired amount, word, or phrase into the box, as indicated.

Control Strip Table

The Control Strip is a collection of small icons that usually appears at the bottom of your iMac's screen. Each of the Control Strip's icons is a shortcut to a frequently used Control Panel or utility, such as the CD/DVD-ROM drive or the sound volume. When the Control Strip is visible, you can access it from virtually anywhere on your iMac. If you don't see your Control Strip, choose the Apple menu⇨Control Panels⇨Control Strip and select Show Control Strip. If you see only the Control Strip tab in the lower-left corner of your screen, click it to expand the strip.

The following table shows the controls on the default Control Strip. Note that if you have additional Control Strip modules, you can add them to the strip by dragging them into the Control Strip Modules folder in the System Folder.

Button	Control	What You Can Do	See
	AppleTalk	Toggle AppleTalk on and off	Part IX
	CD/DVD-ROM	Play a CD, eject the disc	Part III
	Energy Saver	Toggle between energy conservation modes, put your iMac to sleep	Part IX
	File Sharing	Turn file sharing on and off, and show who is connected	Part IX
	Keychain Access	Show keychains, and lock and unlock keychains	Part IX
	Location Manager	Toggle between different locations	Part IX
	Monitor Depth	Toggle between different monitor depth (color) settings	Part IX
	Monitor Resolution	Toggle between different monitor resolution settings	
	Printer	Select a printer	Part VI
	Remote Access	Show Remote Access status, select settings, connect and disconnect	Part IX
	Speakers	Adjust the volume up or down	Part IX
	Sound	Select from available input devices	Part IX
	Web Sharing	Turn Web Sharing on or off	Part IX

The Basics: Powering Up Your iMac

To start your iMac, follow these steps:

1. Press the circular power button at the bottom right of your computer (below the screen). Alternatively, you may press the circular power button on the keyboard.

2. Watch as your iMac goes through its startup sequence, first displaying a "happy Mac" (a computer with a happy face), the "Welcome to Mac OS 9" splash screen, and the march of extension icons across the bottom of the screen.

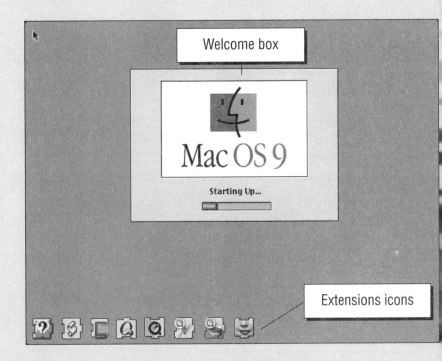

After your desktop appears on your screen, the startup sequence is complete and you may use your iMac.

The Basics: Opening an Application

You can open an application in several different ways:

- ✔ Single-click the application icon on your desktop to select it, and choose File⇨Open.

- ✔ Double-click the application icon on your desktop.

- ✔ Control-click (hold down the Control key as you single-click) the Application icon and choose Open from the contextual menu that appears.

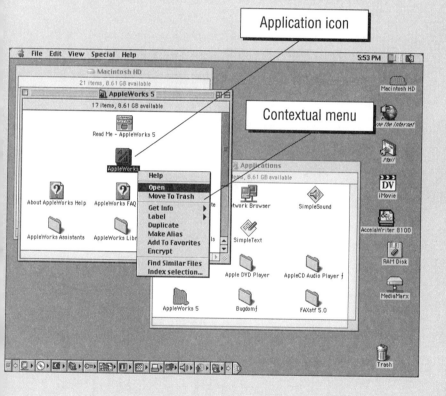

If you add an application to your Apple menu, as described in Part III, you can select it from the Apple menu to open it.

The Basics: Opening Files in AppleWorks

With the AppleWorks application open, you can open a file within it in several ways:

- ✔ Choose File⇨Open.
- ✔ Press ⌘+O.
- ✔ Click the Open button on the toolbar (it looks like an open file folder with a red arrow pointing up).

All these techniques result in the Open dialog box appearing on your screen. Use this dialog box to find the file you want to open. You can use your mouse or keyboard to navigate through your hard drive in the dialog box. When you find your file, single-click it to select it and click Open (or press Return).

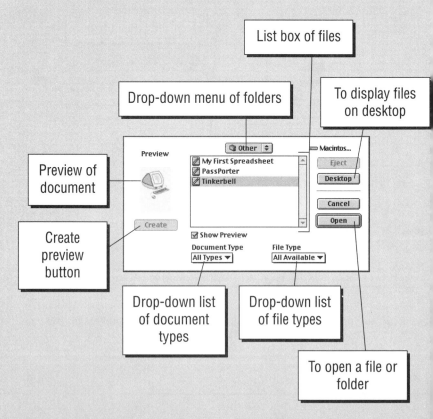

List box of files

Drop-down menu of folders

To display files on desktop

Preview of document

Create preview button

Drop-down list of document types

Drop-down list of file types

To open a file or folder

The Basics: Saving Files in AppleWorks

You should save your files early and often. Here are the ways to save a file in AppleWorks:

✔ Choose File➪Save.

✔ Press ⌘+S.

✔ Click the Save button on the toolbar (it looks like an open file folder with a red arrow pointing down).

The first time you save a new file, your iMac displays the Save dialog box on your screen. Use this dialog box to indicate where you want your file saved, as well as the file type and name. You use the drop-down menu at the top of the dialog box to navigate to a folder higher up in your hard drive hierarchy. The list box helps you move deeper into the hard drive hierarchy. The AppleWorks Save dialog box displays a Save As drop-down menu, which lets you select the format for your saved file. The Document and Stationary radio buttons toggle between a regular file and a template file format. Type your new filename in the text box at the bottom of the window. When you're ready to save your file, click Save or press Return.

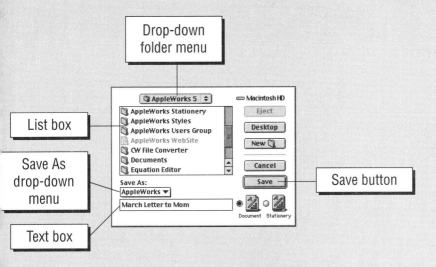

Drop-down folder menu

List box

Save As drop-down menu

Text box

Save button

The Basics: Quitting Applications

After you finish working in an application, you should quit (exit) it. Open applications take up memory, so you don't want to leave an application open if you don't expect to use it soon. Before you quit an application, however, you should save any open files. Here are the ways to quit an application:

✔ Choose File⇨Quit.

✔ Press ⌘+Q.

If you quit an application running open, unsaved files, a dialog box pops up to ask if you want to save changes to your file(s).

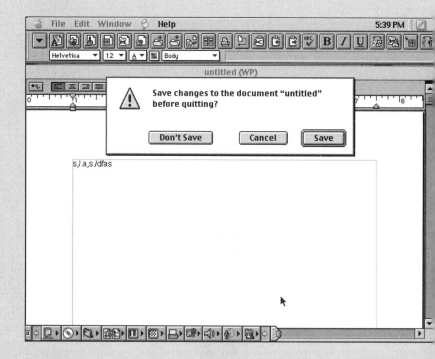

Click Save for the Save dialog box. Click Don't Save if you don't want your work saved. Click Cancel if you don't want to quit the application after all. Note that the dialog box button with a border around it can be activated by pressing the Return key.

What You Can Do

Watch a movie on your iMac DV

If you have an iMac DV model (check your iMac box or documentation), you can play and watch DVD movies on your iMac. Play is simple and quick, and you can adjust the size of the viewing window, turn the volume up or down (or mute it), and choose the point in the movie at which you'd like to start. iMac DV models come with a DVD movie, such as *A Bug's Life* from Disney/Pixar.

1. **Get started by:**

Finding, purchasing, renting a movie on DVD

Inserting the DVD into your iMac, Part III

2. **Work on your project by:**

Opening the Apple DVD Player, Part III

Displaying the Controller, Part III

Starting the movie, Part III

3. **Add finishing touches by:**

Changing the size of the movie window, Part III

Hiding the Controller and/or menu bar for optimum viewing, Part III

What You Can Do

Send a letter via e-mail

Your iMac comes with three preinstalled e-mail applications: Outlook Express, America Online, and Netscape Communicator. Before you can send e-mail, however, you must establish a connection to the Internet with an Internet service provider. After your connection is in place, sending e-mail is fast and easy.

1. Get started by:

Configuring your iMac for Internet access, Part IV

Connecting to your Internet service provider, Part IV

Opening your e-mail application, such as Outlook Express, Part IV

2. Work on your project by:

Opening a new e-mail, Part IV

Typing your recipients e-mail address, Part IV

Typing your letter, Part IV and Part V

Clicking the Send Now button to send your completed e-mail, Part IV

3. Add finishing touches by:

Formatting your letter with font sizes, styles, and alignments, Part IV

Searching for an e-mail address in Sherlock 2, Part IV

Adding attachments, such as a more sophisticated letter created in AppleWorks, Part IV and Part V

What You Can Do

Edit a movie on your iMac DV

iMac DV users can edit movies with the iMovie application. And if you have a DV-capable camcorder, you can import movies you've created and edit those! The iMovie application offers a simple point-and-click interface for easy, fun editing, including sound, music, transitions, and titles.

1. Get started by:

Connecting your DV-capable camcorder to your iMac, Part VIII

Opening the iMovie application, Part VIII

Importing a movie from your camcorder to your iMac, Part VIII

2. Work on your project by:

Adding movie clips to your clip reader, Part VIII

Cropping clips to the desired length, removing unwanted parts, Part VIII

Rearranging clips in the order you wish, Part VIII

3. Add finishing touches by:

Adding a title to a clip, Part VIII

Adding a transition to a clip, Part VIII

Adding music and/or sound to a clip, Part VIII

Part I

Using Your Desktop

Welcome to the iMac! If you're new to the iMac or even computers in general, congratulations are in order — the iMac is a jewel among computers and first in its class. The iMac is easy to learn, especially when you have a good foundation in the basics — which is exactly what the first part of this book offers.

Even if you've had the good sense to use Macintosh computers for years, you may find this part a valuable refresher. It covers the basic skills performed on a day-to-day basis, such as starting up your iMac to display the desktop, moving your pointer, and issuing menu commands.

In this part . . .

Acquainting Yourself with the Desktop

The *desktop,* which is also called the *Finder,* appears on your iMac after powering up. Consider the desktop to be your home base — it offers most of the tools and resources you need to operate your iMac and keep it humming. From the desktop, you can navigate and access your iMac, issue basic commands, organize your files, start programs, and much more.

The desktop fills the entire screen and is usually blue, though you can change the color and style of your desktop. (***See also*** Part VII for how to change the appearance of your desktop.) The following figure shows a common desktop.

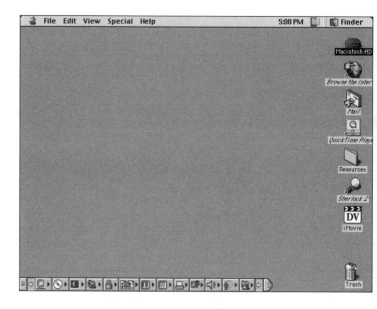

Across the top of the desktop is a *menu bar,* which is a light gray strip with words *(menus).* The desktop is also home to *icons,* which are small pictures that represent files or collections of files. You can find more on menu bars, menus, and icons later in this part.

Clicking Your Mouse

You *click* the button on the mouse to make things happen on your iMac. To click your mouse, press the button once lightly (you hear a click sound) and then release the button (another click sound). If you press and release faster, you hear just one click sound. You can click your mouse in three ways:

- ✔ To *single-click,* position your pointer over a specific icon on your screen and press and release your mouse button just once. Single-clicks are used to *select* items on your desktop, in a menu, in a toolbar, or in a window.

- ✔ To *double-click,* position your pointer over a specific icon on your screen and press and release your mouse button twice in rapid succession. Be sure to keep your pointer in the same location while you double-click — if you move your mouse during the double-click, it probably won't work right. Double-clicks are usually used to activate items on your iMac.

- ✔ To *click-and-drag* (which you may also see referred to as *drag-and-drop*), position your pointer over a specific icon on your screen, click and hold your mouse button, move your mouse to another location, and release your mouse button. You usually see an outline or ghosted image follow your pointer when you're moving your mouse with the button depressed — this allows you to *drop* the item you're *dragging* into a specific location.

Configuring Your iMac with the Mac OS Setup Assistant

The first time you power up your iMac (or install a new operating system), the Mac OS Setup Assistant greets you. You may also use the Setup Assistant to reconfigure certain aspects of your iMac long after you've been using it.

I recommend that you use the Mac OS Setup Assistant to configure important aspects of your computer and to give you practice using your mouse, if needed. Follow these steps to work your way through the Mac OS Setup Assistant:

1. Make the Mac OS Setup Assistant window active. If it is open but isn't the active window, single-click its window. Alternatively, you can select it from the Application menu at the far right end of your menu bar. If the Mac OS Setup Assistant window isn't open at all, you can find the application for it in the Assistants folder on your hard drive — just double-click the Mac OS Setup Assistant icon to launch it.

2. Read the text in the window carefully and, when ready, single-click the right arrow in the lower-right corner of the window. You see the arrow button darken as you press down, indicating that you activated it. The window changes immediately to the next step in the setup process. If you want to go back to the previous window, click the left arrow.

3. Select the keyboard format settings you prefer. One of the keyboard format settings in the list box may already be selected for you — you can tell if it's selected by the darker or colored bar around the text. The item already selected is called the *default*. If you don't want the default setting, move your pointer to the item you do want and single-click it. Click the right arrow again to continue.

4. Type your name and organization by moving your pointer to the first box and typing. You can jump to the next box by pressing the Tab key. Click the right arrow again to continue.

5. Verify the correct time and date. Below the first question are two buttons where you can reply Yes or No. These buttons are called *radio buttons* because they work much like the push buttons on old-fashioned radios — you can depress only one button, and no more than one. Just single-click a radio button to activate it — when it is activated, its circle darkens. Click the right arrow again to continue.

6. Choose the city you live in or a city in the same time zone — this enables your iMac to keep track of your time. To see the entire list of items, single-click the arrows to the right of the list to scroll through the list. Single-click a city name to select it. Click the right arrow again to continue.

7. Indicate if you'd like to use a Simple Finder. As explained in "Setting Desktop Preferences," this limits your options, which you probably don't want. Click the right arrow again to continue.

8. Continue answering the questions as best you can, using the right arrow to continue through the windows. You want to give your computer a name and password (for file sharing and networks), indicate if you want a shared folder (if you don't know what this is, select No), and indicate printer connection and

type (**see also** Part V for printing information) if you know it. If any of these items are inapplicable, do nothing and press the right arrow key to continue.

To learn more about file sharing and networks, **see also** Chapter 14 of *The iMac For Dummies,* by David Pogue and published by IDG Books Worldwide, Inc.

9. When you reach the end of the Mac OS Setup Assistant, apply your choices to your iMac. Click the Go Ahead button to begin setting it up. The Mac OS Setup Assistant keeps you up-to-date as it chugs along.

When finished, you have the option to continue on to the Internet Setup Assistant (click Continue) or stop here (click Cancel). The Internet Setup Assistant helps you configure your iMac for Internet access — **see also** Part III for more information.

Displaying Your Desktop

If your iMac is powered down, you must first power it up to display the desktop. To begin, press the circular power button at the bottom right of your computer (below the screen). You may also press the circular power button on your keyboard, if you have one. Both power buttons have a symbol that looks like a circle with a line through it.

Pushing the power button initiates the startup sequence. You should immediately hear a musical chime and then see a happy-faced Mac appear on your screen. This is followed by the Mac OS logo. (Mac OS, pronounced "Mac Oh Ess," is the name of the operating system software on your iMac.) Icons then march across the bottom of the screen in quick succession — these icons represent your system extensions loading. (**See also** Part VII for more information on system extensions.) In a minute (or less), the startup sequence completes and your iMac displays the desktop on your screen.

If your iMac is already powered up, you can display your desktop in one of two ways:

✓ Move your pointer across your screen until it hovers over a portion of the desktop's background and click the mouse button once. (**See also** "Moving Your Pointer" in this part if you're not sure how to do this.)

✓ Single-click the Application menu (the one at the far right of your menu bar) and select Finder from the drop-down menu. (**See also** "Opening Menus" in this part if you're not sure how to do this.)

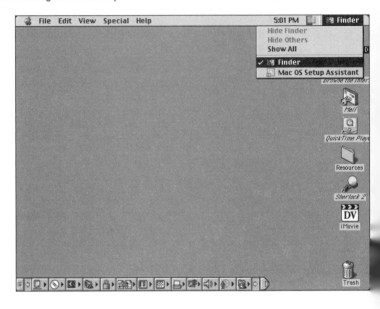

 To confirm that you're on the desktop, check the name of the
Application menu at the far right of your menu bar. If you see the
word Finder and/or a small icon of two blue faces, your iMac is displaying the desktop.

Hiding the Desktop

The desktop is always present in the background when your iMac
is powered up. You can, however, cover up the desktop while
you're working to avoid distractions if you wish. **See also** Part II for
more info.

You can also use your General Controls to disable the Show
Desktop option — doing this hides the items on the desktop when
you are in another application and also prevents you from displaying the desktop if you accidentally click on it. To learn how to do
this, **see also** Part VII.

Moving Your Pointer

Your *pointer,* or *cursor,* is the small, black arrow that you see on
your desktop. Your pointer takes other forms, too, depending on
where you are and what you're doing. To move your pointer, just
move your *mouse* in the direction you want the pointer to go —
your mouse is the small, round device with a cord. If you're not
familiar with how to move a mouse, follow these steps:

1. Place the mouse flat on your work surface with the cord pointing away from you. You can put a *mouse pad* under your mouse
to make it move easier and to protect your work surface, but it
is not necessary.

2. Place your hand on the mouse and position your index finder
lightly on the large button near the top, between the Apple
symbol and the cord. You should be able to press the button
(but don't press it quite yet).

3. Gently grasp the mouse with your thumb on one side and your
remaining fingers on the other side. Feel free to rest your palm
lightly on the top of the desk if that is comfortable for you.

4. Move the mouse around your work surface. Notice that as you
move your mouse, your pointer also moves.

Opening Menus

Menus organize and provide access to the majority of commands
on your iMac. Virtually every piece of software, including the desktop, offers menus with a range of commands. Menus are most
commonly accessed from a *menu bar* at the top of the screen.
Below is the desktop's menu bar.

Each word in the menu bar is the name of an individual menu. Even
the Apple symbol on the far left end is a menu. The menus in a
menu bar change when you open another application (program),
such as Mac OS Setup Assistant.

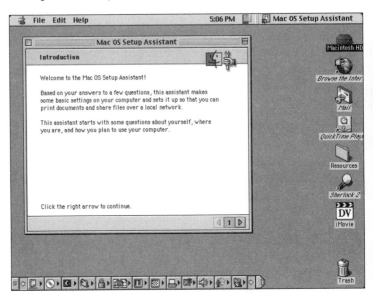

Notice that the first three menus — Apple, File, and Edit — are present in both menu bars. You find these three menus in every menu bar you encounter, and they are always the first three.

Another menu you may see consistently is the *Application menu* at the far right end of the menu bar, but the name changes as you change applications. Note that the Application menu in the desktop menu bar is called *Finder* and in the Mac OS Setup Assistant menu bar bears the name *Mac OS Setup Assistant*. The icon also changes to a small version of the application's icon.

If you'd like more room and less clutter on your menu bar, you can modify the Application menu to display only the icon rather than both the icon and application name. To do this, click-and-drag the small, vertical bar (located on the left of the Application menu) to the right until the name disappears. To expand the menu name, click-and-drag the vertical bar to the right until the full menu name appears.

Displaying menus

To open a menu, follow these steps:

1. Move your pointer until it hovers over the menu name you want to open.

2. Single-click the menu name.

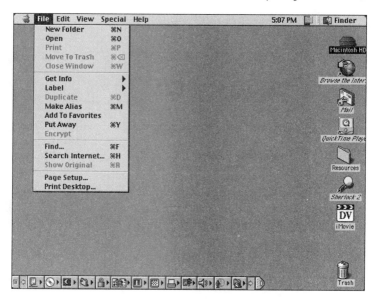

A menu of options drops down and stays open on your screen. You do not have to hold down your mouse button to keep the menu open, though that also works. After you open the menu, you have 15 seconds to move your pointer or issue a command before the menu closes automatically.

When a menu is open, you can open other menus without ever clicking your mouse. Just move your pointer to the left or right along the menu bar. Menus drop down for you as you hover over their menu names and then close up again as you move on.

Viewing submenus

Submenus are new menus that branch off other menus. Your iMac uses submenus to organize related commands together — without submenus, your menus would be much longer and more cluttered. You can recognize a submenu by the small, black triangle that appears to the right of a menu item.

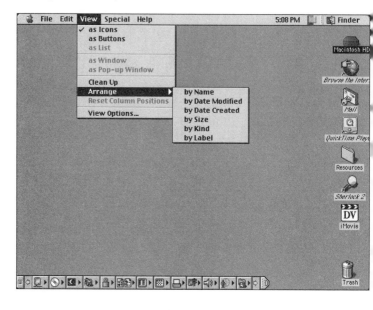

To view a submenu, follow these steps:

1. Open a menu that has a menu item with a submenu arrow.

2. Move your pointer down to a menu item with a submenu but don't click your mouse — instead, allow your pointer to hover over the menu item. The submenu appears beside the menu item after a moment.

3. Slide your pointer across to the submenu. If you accidentally move away from the menu item, just move back and the submenu should reappear.

Submenu commands work the same way as regular menu commands. Some submenu commands even offer keyboard combination shortcuts.

Issuing menu commands

To issue a menu command, follow these steps:

1. Open a menu by single-clicking its name in the menu bar.

2. Move your pointer down the menu. The available menu items highlight as you pass them. Note that items in gray do not highlight — these are inactive menu items.

3. Stop when you reach the command you want — that particular menu item should be highlighted.

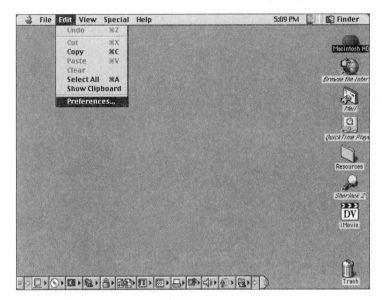

4. Single-click the menu item.

The menu item flashes three times in quick succession to indicate that it was selected and then the command is issued. What happens next depends on which command you issued.

Most menu commands are self-explanatory — the Edit⇨ Preferences . . . command opens the desktop preferences dialog box. If you're not sure about the function of a menu command, refer to Part IX for the Command Reference Guide.

The ellipses (. . .) that follow some menu items indicates that a dialog box of options opens if you issue the command. This is useful to know when you're trying out new commands — if you open a window of options that doesn't interest you, just click the Cancel button or Close box to leave it.

Take a closer look at your menus and you notice that some menu items have a key combination to the right. These key combinations are keyboard shortcuts — press the keys together and you issue the corresponding command. The cloverleaf symbol ⌘ indicates your Command key, which is to the left of your spacebar.

Viewing contextual menus

In addition to menus in menu bars, your iMac offers *contextual menus* throughout the desktop and in many applications. These menus are available in certain places and change based on the location, hence the word *contextual*. Follow these steps to view contextual menus:

1. Position your pointer in a place likely to offer a contextual menu, such as on your desktop, on an icon, in a window, or in a text entry field. Feel free to experiment with any location on your desktop or in any application.

2. Hold down your Control key and single-click your mouse. If a contextual menu is available for that location, it appears beside your pointer.

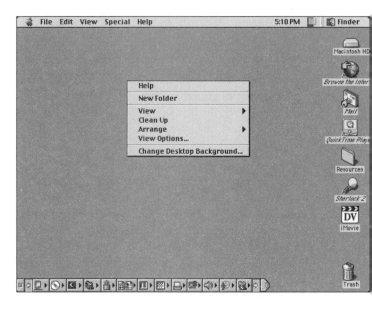

Contextual menus operate in the same way as regular menus in menu bars — just move your pointer down to the desired menu item and single-click. The small black triangles to the right of a menu item indicate a submenu. (*See also* "Viewing submenus" in this part.)

Contextual menus offer useful shortcuts to regular menu commands. Look for them everywhere you go on your iMac — you may even find menu items that aren't available in regular menus.

Putting Your iMac to Sleep

If you want to *blank* your desktop without powering down your iMac, you put your iMac into *sleep mode*. Sleep is a low-power mode that turns off your screen without turning off your iMac or closing any open applications or files. Follow these directions to put your iMac to sleep:

1. Display the desktop. (***See also*** "Displaying Your Desktop" if you're unsure.)

2. Choose Special⇨Sleep.

After you issue the Sleep command, your screen becomes dark. To wake up your iMac, press any key on your keyboard.

Rearranging Desktop Icons

If your iMac is new, you probably only have a handful of icons on your desktop. Over time, however, icons accumulate on the desktop and it can get cluttered. You can manually move and rearrange these icons by clicking-and-dragging them to new locations on your desktop. Your iMac provides another, more efficient method of rearranging desktop icons: the View menu. (If you're unfamiliar with how to use menus, ***see also*** the "Opening Menus" section in this part.)

The fastest way to rearrange your desktop icons is the Clean Up command. Click once on the desktop to activate it and then choose View⇨Clean Up to arrange your desktop icons into neat columns.

The Clean Up command doesn't have any effect if you have your desktop View Options set to Always Snap to Grid. (***See also*** Part IX for details on View Options.)

You can also sort your icons alphabetically by name, date, size, and so on. First choose Views⇨Arrange and then select your criteria from the submenu. (***See also*** "Viewing submenus" in this part.)

You may also choose to have your icons appear as buttons rather than standard icons. This is both good and bad. Normally, you have to double-click icons to open or activate them, but if they are buttons instead, you only need to single-click them. On the other hand, you can't click-and-drag buttons the way you can icons. If you want to try buttons, choose View⇨as Buttons. If you don't like the buttons, just choose Views⇨as Icons to change them back.

Setting Desktop Preferences

You have a range of options for the look and feel of your desktop. To set your preferences, choose Edit⇨Preferences.

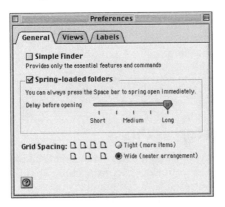

The three tabs across the top of the Preferences window — General, Views, and Labels — let you switch between the three preference sets with a single click.

General preferences offer the following options:

✔ *Simple Finder* offers a leaner version of your desktop with fewer menu items. This is primarily useful when setting up an iMac for a young child or someone who is easily confused by all the choices. I don't recommend you use a Simple Finder for yourself, as it will limit the commands available to you.

✔ *Spring-loaded folders,* when selected, instructs your iMac to automatically open desktop windows when you click-and-drag an item and let it hover over the icon or folder. This lets you move one item into another without manually opening all the icons/folders. You can also set the delay before a folder automatically opens — to change the delay, click-and-hold the indicator, and then move your pointer in either direction. (*See also* Part II for more detail on moving files and folders.)

✔ *Grid Spacing* enables you to choose between a tight or wide grid for your desktop icon arrangement. Your iMac uses this preference when you use the Clean Up command or Always Snap to Grid in View Options.

Views and Labels preferences are useful tools for sorting and organizing windows. *See also* Part II for more info on these preferences.

Shutting Down Your iMac

Powering down your iMac completely deactivates your desktop as well as any applications you may be using. Before you turn off your iMac, save and close any work and quit all open applications.

You can initiate the shutdown sequence in one of two ways:

✔ Display your desktop and choose Special⇨Shut Down. When you do this, your iMac immediately shuts down — your screen goes blank, and your hard drive stops spinning.

✔ Press the power button on your keyboard. When you do this, a small *dialog box* appears on your desktop and asks you if you're sure you want to shut down your computer now.

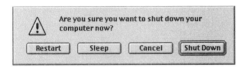

The dialog box presents four options: Restart, Sleep, Cancel, and Shut Down. (Restart means to shut down and immediately start your iMac back up.) Single-click the Shut Down button or press the Return key. Note that the Shut Down button is outlined — whenever you see a button like this in other dialog boxes, you can press the Return key on your keyboard to activate it.

 Avoid shutting down your iMac by simply turning off your surge suppressor/power strip or unplugging the iMac's power cord. Doing this can lead to trouble later on. The shutdown sequence is necessary to the health and happiness of your iMac.

Using the Launcher

You know that remote control you have at home? Your desktop is your home base, so you also have a kind of remote control built-in to your iMac: the Launcher.

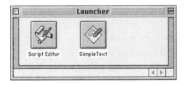

The *Launcher* helps you keep your desktop organized and access your favorite files, applications, and folders faster and easier. It gets its name from the fact that you only need to single-click one of its buttons to launch it.

Launching the Launcher

To access your Launcher, choose the Apple menu (the one on the far left of your menu bar), choose Control Panels, and then choose Launcher from the submenu.

Adding items to the Launcher

To add favorite files, applications, or folders to the Launcher, click-and-drag the item you want to add to the Launcher window and release your mouse button. A new button with the item's icon should appear in the Launcher, ready for you to use.

Removing items from the Launcher

To remove something from the Launcher, hold down the Option key while you click-and-drag the item out of the Launcher and over to the Trash icon on your desktop. This removes the button (and doesn't delete the item itself from your hard drive).

Configuring the Launcher

You can create different sets of items in your Launcher for even more organization. Follow these steps to create a new Launcher set:

1. Locate and open your Launcher Items folder, which is located inside your System Folder.

2. Choose File⇨New Folder to create a new folder in the Launcher Items folder. A new, untitled folder appears and is ready to accept a title.

3. Type in a name for your new folder. To name your folder, first press Option+8 to create the bullet (•) character, and then type an appropriate name for your Launcher set, such as Games or Work Files. The bullet character tells your iMac to use this new folder as a Launcher set, so it is important that the name of your folder begins with this character.

Now, when you open your Launcher again, set buttons appear at the top of the Launcher window. Click a button to change to a different Launcher set. Repeat the above procedure as many times as necessary to create more Launcher sets.

You can change the size of your Launcher buttons. Just hold down the ⌘ key and click any nonbutton area inside the Launcher window. A small menu appears with the following options: Small Buttons, Medium Buttons, and Large Buttons. Choose one, and your buttons change immediately.

Part II

Navigating Folders and Windows

Not only is your iMac visually striking, lightning fast, and extremely powerful, but it's also a versatile and spacious file cabinet. Your iMac organizes its many files into *folders,* which are simply containers for files and other folders. You can organize your computer files into folders and then open them to reveal windows that display their contents. This part shows you how to navigate the folders and windows.

In this part . . .

Closing Folders and Windows

Opening a folder produces an open window (**see also** "Opening Folders and Windows" later in this part if you're unfamiliar with how to open them). To close an open folder's window, and thus close the folder, simply click the Close box in the upper-left corner of the folder's window.

Close box

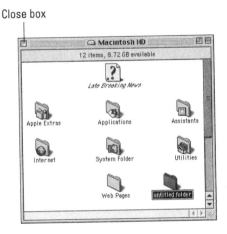

Alternately, press ⌘+W or control-click anywhere in an open window to produce a contextual menu with a Close Window option.

Collapsing Windows

Collapsing windows means to reduce a window to its title bar (the strip at the top of a window that includes its name). It works a bit like a window shade — you collapse a window and its "shade" rolls up, uncollapse and its "shade" rolls back down. Collapsing windows is helpful when you want to get a window out of your way without actually closing it.

To collapse a window, click its Collapse box in the upper-right corner of the window (the box with two horizontal lines in its center). To uncollapse (expand) the window, just click the Collapse box again.

Collapse box

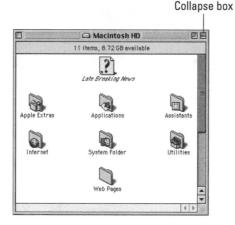

To collapse (or expand) all open windows on the desktop or in an application at the same time, just hold down the Option key as you click the Collapse box.

If you find yourself frequently collapsing windows, the iMac offers a faster way to do it. Here's how:

1. Choose the Apple menu⇨Control Panels⇨Appearance.

2. Click the Options tab at the far right of the window.

3. Enable the "Double-click title bar to collapse windows" option and close the Appearance control panel window.

Now you can double-click a title bar to collapse and expand windows. And if you hold down the Option key while double-clicking a title bar, you can collapse or expand all windows on the desktop or in an application at the same time.

Creating Folders

Creating a new folder on your iMac is surprisingly simple. Follow these steps:

1. Navigate to the location on your hard drive where you want to place a new folder. This can be at the top level of your hard drive or within another folder.

2. Choose File⇨New Folder or press ⌘+N. Alternately, control-click in the location you want your new folder to appear and choose New Folder from the resulting contextual menu.

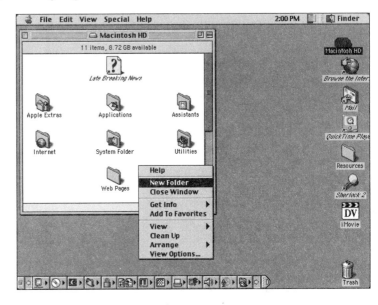

3. After the new untitled folder appears, begin typing a new name immediately. If you accidentally click elsewhere before you give your new folder a name, see the section "Renaming Folders" later in this part.

Deleting Folders

To delete a folder, click-and-drag it to the Trash icon in the lower-right corner of your desktop. A ghost image of the folder follows your pointer — release the mouse when the Trash icon darkens. Your folder disappears from its original location and the Trash icon changes to show that it contains something (unless you already had something in the Trash).

Alternately, you can control-click a folder and select Move to Trash from the contextual menu.

Deleting a folder also deletes all the items within the folder.

See also "Emptying the Trash" to learn how to permanently delete folders.

These techniques also work on files.

Duplicating Folders

To make a copy of a folder, select the folder and choose File⇨Duplicate. Alternately, you can press ⌘+D or control-click and select Duplicate from the contextual menu. The Duplicate command makes a copy of a folder and all its contents. The duplicate folder appears in the same folder as the copied folder — even its name is the same, though the duplicate folder has the word *copy* appended to the end of its name.

If you want to duplicate a folder and have it appear in another location, hold down the Option key and click-and-drag the folder icon to the desired location. When you release the mouse button, a copy of the folder appears.

If you have more than one hard drive (or partition), simply copying a folder to another hard drive or partition causes it to duplicate itself.

These techniques work on files, too.

Emptying the Trash

When the Trash contains items you're ready to permanently delete, choose Special⇨Empty Trash. Alternately, you can control-click the Trash and select Empty Trash.

After you choose to empty the trash, your iMac informs you of the number of items in the Trash and the amount of disk space it occupies, asking you if you're sure you want to remove the item(s) permanently. If you are sure, click OK or press the Return key (otherwise, click the Cancel button to stop the process). Your iMac deletes the items in the Trash and changes the Trash icon back (the lid is put on the Trash again).

If you get tired of your iMac always asking if you want to empty the Trash, you can disable this warning. Follow these steps:

1. Select the Trash icon.

2. Press ⌘+I. The Trash Info dialog box appears.

3. Click the Warn Before Emptying option so that the check box is unchecked.

4. Close the window.

From now on, you and anyone else using your iMac can empty the Trash without confirming it. I recommend you remove this warning only if you feel confident that you or someone else won't accidentally choose Empty Trash.

Finding a Folder

Here's how to find a folder that's missing:

1. Press ⌘+F or choose File➪Find. The Sherlock 2 dialog box appears.

2. Type the name of the folder. If you're not sure of the exact folder name, type a word most likely to be in the name.

3. Click the Magnifying Glass button or the Find button.

Sherlock 2 displays the matching results in the window below. You should recognize a folder by its folder icon.

This technique work on files, too. More information on Sherlock is available in Parts IV and XI.

Getting Information on a Folder

You can get very particular information on each and every folder on your iMac. Here's how to do it:

1. Select a folder by single-clicking its icon. Alternately, you can simply make a folder's window active.

2. Choose File⇨Get Info⇨General Information, or press ⌘+I. Alternately, you can control-click anywhere on the folder's icon or in a folder's open window and choose Get Info⇨General Information from the contextual menu.

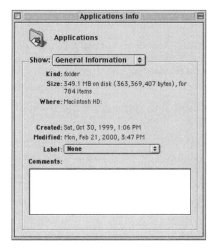

This technique works on files, as well.

Information for a folder appears in a new window on your screen. The window displays the folder's icon, name, kind, size, location, creation date, modification date, label, and comments (if any).

You can change several things in the information window, including the icon, name, label, and comments. The latter three are easy — just type a new name, select a new label from the drop-down menu, or type comments in the Comments field. To change a folder's icon, **see also** "Replacing Folder Icons" in this part.

Moving Folders

To move a folder, simply click-and-drag it from its original location to a new location and release the mouse button. After you release the mouse button, the folder disappears from its original location and reappears in its new location.

If you want to move a folder into a nested folder (a folder within a folder), you don't have to open the nested folder first. Just click-and-drag it over the folder that contains the folder you want to move it to and wait one second. The folder opens automatically to reveal its contents. This is called *spring-loading* (**see also** Part I for more details). If your folder is nested several levels down, you can continue to hold down your mouse button while you move the item onto folder after folder until you find the one you seek.

To move several folders at a time, first select all the folders you wish to move by holding down the Shift key and selecting each folder individually. Alternatively, if the folders you wish to select are all next to one another, you can use the following selection technique:

1. Position your pointer at the far edge of the group of folders (but not directly on a folder).

2. Click-and-drag to the other side of the grouping. Your iMac displays a gray rectangle as you drag to show the area being selected.

3. After you select the folders, position your pointer over one of the selected folders.

4. Click-and-drag the folders into their new location and release the mouse button.

These techniques work on files, too.

Moving Windows

Position your pointer on the gray border around the four sides of a window, keeping away from the Close, Zoom, Collapse, and Resize boxes. Now click-and-drag your pointer — a ghost of your window follows your pointer. Release your mouse button when the window is in the location you desire.

If you want to move a folder that is currently open, follow these steps:

1. Locate the folder's window.

2. Position your pointer over the small icon in its title bar (to the left of its name).

3. Click-and-drag the small folder icon to the desired location and release the mouse button.

Navigating Folders

Folders often contain files, because the purpose of folders is to organize files. In the same vein, folders are often located in another folder, which may in turn be located in yet another folder. This *nesting* can be hard to navigate if you aren't familiar with this organizational scheme or the techniques to master it.

If you have an open folder and wish to know where it is located, follow these directions:

1. Position your pointer on the folder's title at the top of its window.

2. Control-click on the title bar — you see the path that leads to the open window. You can choose a location from this menu to display it (open its window) on your desktop.

In the figure, you see the Bugdom folder is located in the Applications folder, which is on the hard drive named Macintosh HD.

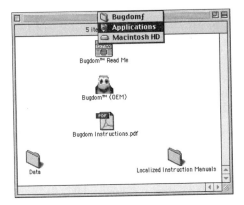

Opening Folders and Windows

Folders are generally closed when you first encounter them. To open a folder, double-click the folder's icon. Alternately, you can choose File⇨Open, press ⌘+O, or control-click and choose Open from the contextual menu. You can use these techniques to open files, too.

An open folder produces a window and displays its contents as either icons, lines of text, or buttons. **See also** "Sorting Folders and Windows" to learn how to change the way an open window displays its contents.

If you'd like to open a folder and close the folder that it's in at the same time, hold down the Option key as you open a folder. This automatically closes the originating folder at the same time it opens the new folder.

Renaming Folders

Renaming folders is simple — and often necessary to good organization. Here's how to do it:

1. Click once on the name of a folder and wait a second. The name of the folder is highlighted to indicate that you can type over it.

2. Type a new name. Alternately, you may position your pointer at a specific point in the name to modify or add new text to the existing name.

3. Press the Return key or click anywhere on the desktop (other than the folder's name or icon) to set the new name.

You can use this technique to rename files, too.

If you click a folder name and the name isn't highlighted, you are not allowed to rename it. This may be because you locked or encrypted the folder or because the folder is being shared across a network. *See also* Part XI for more information on locking and encrypting; *see also* Chapter 14 of *The iMac For Dummies,* 2nd Edition, by David Pogue and published by IDG Books Worldwide, Inc., for more information on networking and file sharing.

Replacing Folder Icons

For the most part, you won't want to replace a folder icon — the standard icon of a file folder is easy to recognize. If you do want to change it, either to customize your iMac or make the icon stand out, here's how to do it:

1. Locate the icon that you want to use. This icon may be from an existing folder or file on your iMac, or it may be on the Internet (*see also* Part IV for information on connecting to the Internet).

2. Copy the new icon to your Clipboard. If the icon is on another folder or file on your hard drive, select the icon, press ⌘+I, select the icon that appears in the upper-left corner of the Get Info dialog box, and press ⌘+C.

3. Click once on the folder for which you want to replace the icon and press ⌘+I.

4. Single-click the icon in the upper-left corner of the Get Info dialog box.

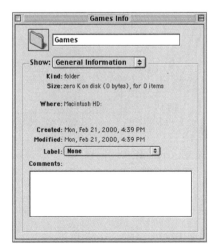

5. Press ⌘+V to paste the new icon from the clipboard.

6. Close the dialog box. You see your new icon on the folder.

If you simply want to change the color of a folder icon, select the icon, choose File⇨Label, and select a label. And if you want to change the colors of the labels themselves, choose Edit⇨ Preferences, click the Labels tab, and click a label color to choose a new one. Keep in mind that changing a label color also changes the color of all items that have been assigned that label across your system.

These techniques work on files, too.

Resizing Windows

To resize a window, begin by positioning your pointer over the Resize box in the lower-right corner of a window. The Resize box has three diagonal lines in it.

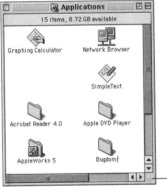

—Resize box

Click-and-drag the Resize box, noting that a gray outline follows your pointer to show you the new window size. Release the mouse button when the window is at your preferred size.

Scrolling Windows

If a folder's contents cannot be shown in their entirety in the open window, *scroll bars* appear along the right side and/or bottom of the open window. You can use the controls on the scroll bars to move through the contents of the window, allowing you to see everything in it. To use the scroll bars, click the arrows to move up, down, left, and right.

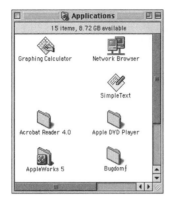

Another way to scroll is by positioning your pointer over the solid box in the scroll bar. This scroll box has three horizontal lines on it and its size is relative to how much of the window is already being displayed (the larger the box, the less there is to scroll). Just click-and-drag the scroll box and the contents of the window scroll up or down, left or right, as you move. Release the mouse button when the window shows the items you want to see. You can also click above or below the box in the scroll bar to scroll the window.

Looking for a faster way to scroll? Try positioning your pointer in an empty part of the window, holding down the ⌘ key while you click and hold down your mouse button. While continuing to hold down your mouse button, move your pointer. The window moves with your pointer, allowing you to display other parts of the window.

Sorting Folders and Windows

You can use the View menu (**see also** Part I) to change the look and feel of a window. For example, you may want to change a window from Icon view to List view. After you display a window as a list, you can easily sort its contents. Just click the column labels near the top of a window in List view and the list re-sorts itself alphabetically based on that column's contents. Use this technique to sort a folder's contents by name (default), date modified, size, kind, and so on.

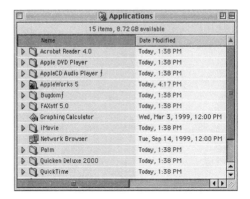

You can also control which columns are displayed in List view by choosing View⇨View Options and selecting the items you want from the Show Columns list in the resulting window.

To sort items in reverse order, click the arrow at the far-right end of the column bar in a window that is being displayed in List view. Once clicked, the arrow changes direction to show that it has reversed the order. Click the arrow again to return to the previous ordering.

To change the size of the columns to see your folder's information better, follow these steps:

1. Position your pointer at the right end of the column you want to resize. Your pointer changes to a horizontal bar with two arrows on either side.

2. When your pointer changes, click-and-drag your pointer to resize the column.

3. Release the mouse button when the column is at the desired size. If you later decide you want your columns back at their original sizes, choose View⇨Reset Column Positions.

Zooming Windows

Zooming a window means to increase or decrease its size without using the Resize box. Click once on a window's Zoom box (the box in the upper-right corner with the smaller box inside of it) to zoom out (enlarge) your window.

Zoom box

Click the Zoom box on the same window again to zoom back in to the window's original size. Zooming is an alternative to resizing and scrolling (if there aren't too many items to display in the window, of course).

Mastering Discs and Files

Your iMac may not have a floppy disk drive, but it certainly has another kind of disc drive: a CD-ROM or DVD-ROM drive. With it, you can install new software programs, listen to a concerto on an audio CD, or watch the latest movie on DVD. Learning to insert, read, use, eject, and protect these discs is essential if you plan to use them.

Beyond discs, your iMac also has files, and plenty of them. In many ways, working with files is much like working with folders, but many important differences exist, such as encrypting and searching.

This part introduces you to the more technical side of your iMac: its discs and data.

In this part . . .

Acquainting Yourself with CD-ROM and DVD-ROM Discs

CD-ROM stands for *compact disc-read only memory,* which means that you can read the information on the disc but you cannot record (or write) to the disc. In other words, you can copy files from the disc to your hard drive, but you cannot copy files from your hard drive to the CD-ROM. You probably already knew that, though.

How about DVD-ROMs? DVD stands for *digital video disc* and is also read-only. DVD-ROMs most typically hold movies or graphic-intensive games, because they can store considerably more information than a CD-ROM.

Your iMac may or may not have the ability to play DVD-ROMs, but all iMacs can read CD-ROMs. How do you know whether you can do DVDs in addition to CDs? First, check what model of iMac you bought — if you see "DV" in the model name, such as in "iMac DV Special Edition," then you have a DVD-ROM drive. If you can't remember which model you bought, no problem. Follow these steps:

1. Choose the Apple menu⇨Apple System Profiler.

2. Click the Devices and Volumes tab at the top of the window.

3. Look for a DVD-ROM or CD-ROM device.

If your iMac has a DVD-ROM drive, then it can also read CD-ROMs. On the other hand, if you have a CD-ROM drive, you cannot read DVD-ROMs. Don't worry, however — this section is for both CD-ROMs and DVD-ROMs.

Inserting discs

The method of inserting discs depends on the iMac model. If you see an oblong button about an inch long below the word *iMac* on your computer, you have a tray-loading CD-ROM drive. If you see a colored slot about five and a half inches long below the word *iMac,* then you have a slot-loading CD-ROM or DVD-ROM drive. (All iMac DVD-ROM drives are slot-loading.) I describe each of these two drives in turn.

To insert a disc into a tray-loading CD-ROM drive, follow these steps:

1. Open the tray by pushing the oblong button directly below the word *iMac* on the front of your computer.

2. Gently pull out the tray until the tray stops.

3. Remove a disc from its sleeve or case.

4. Place the disc in the tray (label up, shiny side down) and press the disc's center down until it snaps onto the spindle.

5. Gently push the tray back into your computer. You hear a whirring noise as the disc spins up.

To insert a disc into a slot-loading CD-ROM or DVD-ROM drive, follow these steps:

1. Remove a disc from its sleeve or case.

2. Insert the disc into the long slot below the word *iMac* on the front of your computer, pushing gently until the iMac begins pulling in the disc. (You need to push it in only about an inch yourself.) You hear a whirring noise as the disc spins up.

If all goes well, the disc's icon appears on your desktop.

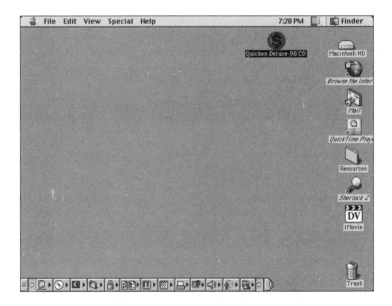

Usually the icon opens by itself and a window appears on your desktop. If it doesn't open, or if you can't see the window, just double-click the disc icon. (It often, but not always, looks like a round disc.)

Reading CD-ROM discs

After a CD-ROM disc is inserted and *mounted* on your desktop, its data is available to read, run, install, and so on. If you inserted a

CD-ROM disc, just double-click the appropriate items in the disc window like you would anything else on your desktop. Note the small padlock symbol and crossed-out pencil in the upper-left corner of your disc's window — these symbols indicate the disc is locked and can only be read from, not written to.

In the figure, the Quicken CD-ROM window presents a "Double-click to Quicken 98" icon, which launches the installation program.

Listening to audio discs

Your CD-ROM or DVD-ROM drive can also play music! To listen to an audio disc, insert a music disc the same way you insert any other CD-ROM or DVD-ROM disc (*see also* "Inserting discs" for details). Your iMac automatically recognizes the music data and begins playing the first track. You can double-click the audio CD icon to view the tracks — double-clicking a track icon opens the AppleCD Audio Player and plays that particular track. Use the Audio Player like a regular CD player to pause, fast forward, reverse, and so on. Adjust the volume with the slider on the right or plug earphones into the jack on the front of your iMac.

You may also open the AppleCD Audio Player at anytime. It may be located in your Apple menu or in your Applications folder. *See also* "Finding Files" in this part for help locating the AppleCD Audio Player.

To learn more about the AppleCD Audio Player, check out *The iMac For Dummies* by David Pogue.

Playing DVD-ROM discs

If you have an iMac DV model, you can play DVD-ROM movies in your iMac, too! In fact, you probably received a free DVD with your iMac — mine came with *A Bug's Life*. Here's how to play a DVD-ROM:

1. Choose the Apple menu⇨Apple DVD Player. You see a blank viewer window and a round controller panel that reads "No Disc."

2. Remove the disc from its sleeve or case and insert it into your drive.

3. After you insert the disc and the controller panel reads "Stopped," press the Play button on the controller (the big arrow pointing to the right at the bottom).

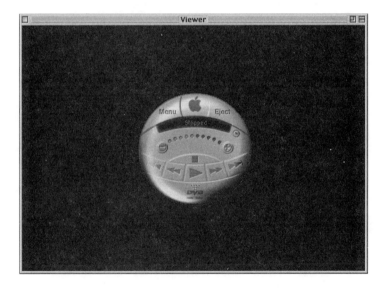

The Controller loads and then plays the DVD. If the Controller is in your way, you can choose Window⇨Hide Controller. Depending on the sophistication of the DVD you've inserted, either the movie begins immediately or you see a variety of options. Many DVDs offer extra goodies, such as outtakes and trailers, in addition to the movie itself. *A Bug's Life* offers outtakes and a mini-story ("Geri's Game"). You may also be able to choose closed captioning (*A Bug's Life* offers English closed captioning for the hearing impaired), as well as other languages and sound mixes, such as different versions of Dolby sound output. Most DVDs let you skip to different *chapters* of the story, so that you can start over from where you stopped last or replay your favorite scene.

Ejecting discs

To eject a disc, follow these steps:

1. Close all open windows, files, and programs on the disc. If you're playing a DVD movie, quit out of the DVD Player.

2. Click-and-drag the disc icon to the trash. Don't worry — you're not removing any data from the disc (remember, you can only read a disc's data, not change it). You can also choose Special⇨Eject, File⇨Put Away, or press ⌘+Y or ⌘+E.

If you have a tray-loading drive, the tray pops open again, and you can remove the disc. If you have a slot-loading drive, your iMac spits out the disc part way — put your index finger through the spindle hole and a thumb on the edge to pull the disc the rest of the way out.

Ejected discs disappear from your desktop, and you cannot access their data unless you copied it to your hard drive or until you re-insert the disc.

Protecting discs

Discs are fairly sturdy and usually take a long time to wear out, but they do require careful handling. Be careful not to touch the underside of a disc, because fingerprints and dust can confuse the drive. Instead, hold the disc by the edges. This can be a challenge when inserting or ejecting a disc, but with careful attention, you can do it. When finished with a disc, always put it back in its sleeve or case to protect it. Keep discs in their sleeves or cases until you need them.

Copying Files

To copy a file to another folder on your hard drive, follow these steps:

1. Locate the file you want to copy.

2. Hold down the Option key.

3. Click-and-drag the file to the location to which you'd like it copied.

4. Release the mouse button and then the Option key.

This action produces an exact copy of the file in the new location.

If you want to copy a file to a different disk or partition, simply click-and-drag the file to the other disk or partition. A copy is automatically created for you when you release the mouse button.

These techniques work for copying folders, too (*see also* Part II).

Deleting Files

To delete a file, click-and-drag it to the Trash icon in the lower-right corner of your desktop. Alternately, you can control-click a folder and choose Move to Trash from the contextual menu.

See also Part II to learn how to permanently delete files.

Duplicating and Aliasing Files

To duplicate a file in the same folder, select it on your desktop and choose File⇨Duplicate or press ⌘+D. Alternately, you can control-click the file and select Duplicate from the contextual menu that appears. Either way, a new file appears with the same name as the original, but with the word *copy* appended to the end. This new file appears to the lower right of the original file (in Icon view) or immediately below it (in List view).

If you'd prefer to simply make a shortcut to the original file and place that shortcut somewhere else, you may want to make an *alias* of the file instead. Here's how to make an alias:

1. Select the file you want to make an alias of.

2. Choose File⇨Make Alias or press ⌘+M. Alternately, you can control-click on the file and choose Make Alias from the contextual menu.

An alias of the file appears next to the original file, but its name is in italics and the word *alias* is appended to the end. Double-clicking an alias file works the same as clicking the file itself.

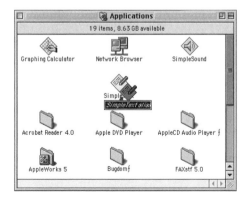

You can move this alias wherever you want, including into your Apple menu for quick access (**see also** "Moving Files" for details on how to do this).

A quick way to make an alias in a new location is to hold down the Option and ⌘ keys and then click-and-drag the file to the desired location. When you release the mouse and keys, a new alias appears in the location to which you dragged the original file.

Encrypting Files

Encrypting files, which is a new feature with Mac OS 9, enables you to protect your sensitive files with passwords. If this is your first time encrypting a file, follow these steps:

1. Choose File⇨Encrypt. The Apple File Security application launches.

2. Choose File⇨Open and select the file you would like to encrypt. Note that files in the System Folder cannot be encrypted.

3. Type a passphrase of at least five characters as protection; choose something you can remember. Type it again to confirm it.

4. Decide whether to include the passphrase in your Keychain (a new feature of Mac OS 9). Then, if you forget your passphrase, you can open your Keychain Control Panel to find it. Note that you must choose a password for your Keychain Control Panel, and this one you need to memorize.

5. Click Encrypt (or press Return).

If you enabled the Add to Keychain option but haven't yet set one up, your iMac asks you if you want to create a keychain. If you do, click Create.

In the future, you can simply select the file you wish to encrypt and choose File⇨Encrypt to secure it with a passphrase.

 After you encrypt a file, a small key symbol appears on its icon and you must type in the passphrase before you can open the file. If you can't remember your passphrase but know that you stored it in your keychain, choose the Apple menu⇨Control Panels⇨Key Chain

Access, unlock your keychain with your master passphrase, and look up the item's own passphrase. Be careful to never lose your keychain's passphrase, however, or your files will be inaccessible.

Finding Files

Your iMac comes with a powerful system for finding files and folders: Sherlock. Apple beefed up Sherlock in Mac OS 9, calling it Sherlock 2. In principle, the two versions work similarly, though Sherlock 2 provides more features and options. This section describes Sherlock 2, but users of the earlier version can use the same basic concepts to find files.

If you're looking for a wayward file somewhere on your iMac, follow these steps:

1. Choose File⇨Find or press ⌘+F. You can also choose the Apple menu⇨Sherlock 2.

2. Type the name of the file or a word in the name of the file as you remember it.

3. Click the magnifying glass (Find) button.

Sherlock 2 searches your iMac and displays the matching results in the bottom half of the window. If you see what you're looking for in the results, you can open it from there with a simple double-click.

If you can't find your file with a simple search, follow these steps:

1. Open Sherlock 2 as described earlier.

2. Click the Edit . . . button at the far right side of the Sherlock 2 window. The More Search Options dialog box opens to reveal a wide range of criteria that you can use to find your file. For example, you can find only files created in the last day or files less than 50 kilobytes in size.

3. Select the option that best meets your need and click OK to close the window.

4. Type a name (if the criteria you chose requires it) or leave the text field blank (if a name isn't necessary).

5. Click the magnifying glass (Find) button.

Another search technique is to look inside files, in the event you simply cannot remember the name of a file or perhaps gave it a bad name. To search file contents, follow these steps:

1. Open Sherlock 2 as described earlier.

2. Choose Find⇨Index Volumes or press ⌘+L.

3. Select the Macintosh HD (or the name of your hard drive, if you changed it) and then click Create Index.

Note that the first time you index an entire hard drive can take some time, and you may prefer to do it later (use the Schedule button to set this up).

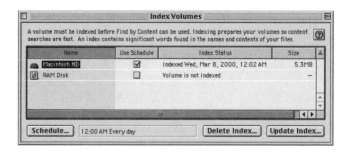

4. After your hard drive is indexed, return to the main Sherlock window and type the word or phrase you want to search for in your files.

5. Click the Contents radio button to select it.

6. Click the magnifying glass (Find) button to begin searching, displaying results in the bottom half of the window.

Searching the contents of your indexed files should go swiftly after your hard drive is indexed. Keep in mind, however, that the more recent your hard drive index, the more likely you are to find what you're seeking.

 You can set your iMac to regularly index your hard drive so that the index is always up-to-date. Use the Schedule button to set up automatic indexing.

Moving Files

To move a file, simply click-and-drag it from its original location to a new location and release the mouse button. After you release the mouse button, the file disappears from its original location and reappears in its new location.

You can move a file into the Apple menu for easy access, but consider moving an alias of the file rather than the original. If you move the original file to the Apple menu, you may later forget where you put it, which may cause all sorts of problems. To create an alias of a file in the Apple menu, follow these steps:

1. Locate the Apple Menu Items folder inside the System Folder, which is at the top level of your Macintosh HD.

2. Locate the file you want to move, hold down the Option and ⌘ keys while you click-and-drag the file over to the Apple Menu Items folder. This action creates an alias of the file in the Apple Menu Items folder.

3. Display the Apple menu. You can see an alias of the file on the Apple menu.

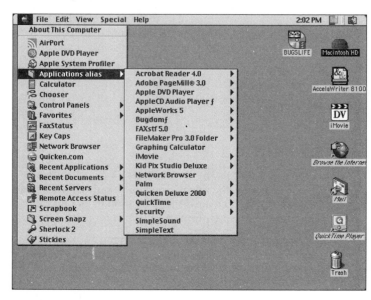

 For greater ease in navigating your hard drive, create an alias of Macintosh HD and place the alias in the Apple Menu Items folder. Now your entire hard drive is accessible through the Apple menu; you can navigate it using submenus.

If you want to move a file into a nested folder (a folder within a folder) without having to open each folder manually, *see also* Part II.

Opening Files

You can open files in several ways. Single-click a file and choose File⇨Open (or press ⌘+O). You can also double-click a file to open it. Alternately, you can control-click on a file and choose Open from the contextual menu.

If the file you opened is an application file (program), opening it causes the application to start up and, often, display a new blank document. If the file is a document file, opening it launches the application that created it and then displays the document within the application.

Part IV

Using the Internet and Sending Faxes

Did you know the *i* in *iMac* stands for Internet? That's right —
you have an Internet Mac. That means your computer is particularly adept at connecting to and making the most of the Internet.
Whether that means surfing the Web or checking e-mail, you can do
it. In fact, Sherlock 2, the enhanced search utility that comes with
Mac OS 9, is particularly good at ferreting out information from the
Internet.

In addition to your ability to connect to the Internet with ease, your
iMac comes with fax software. With it, you can send faxes to and
receive faxes from other fax machines (and the people behind
them). You can also create custom cover pages, store fax numbers,
and keep an archive of faxes sent and received.

In this part . . .

Connecting to the Internet

Your iMac comes ready to connect to the Internet with its built-in modem. A *modem* is a device that translates, sends, and receives data over normal telephone lines. Modems convert the digital data on your computer into analog information that can be sent through the lines and then convert it back again on the receiving end. The faster your modem can do this, the faster your connection and the happier you are. The speed of a modem is measured by its *baud rate*. Your modem is capable of achieving baud rates up to 56K (pronounced "fifty-six-kay"). You aren't likely to actually achieve speeds of 56K, however, because the telephone lines themselves slow transmission speeds with static and other noise.

Connecting your phone line

To attach a telephone line cable between your iMac and a wall outlet, follow these steps:

1. Locate the telephone line cable that came with your iMac, or purchase a longer cable if you need it. (Look for a standard RJ-11 cable at an electronics or hardware store.)

2. Plug one end of the telephone cable into the modem jack on your iMac. Your iMac's modem jack is located on the access panel on the lower-right of the computer. The jack is identified by a small phone symbol.

3. Plug the other end of the telephone cable into the nearest telephone wall jack. If your surge suppressor has telephone jacks, use them — be sure to connect another telephone line cable between the surge suppressor and the wall jack, too. If your wall jack already has a telephone line cable plugged into it, purchase a *splitter* from your local hardware store; it allows your two telephone cables to share one jack.

 If you have a PBX, Merlin, or another proprietary phone system, you need a phone with a *data jack* or have a regular phone line installed.

Using Internet Setup Assistant

If you did not complete the setup procedures the first time you started up your iMac, follow these steps to use Internet Setup Assistant:

1. Open Internet Setup Assistant from the Assistants folder on your Macintosh HD.

2. When Internet Assistant asks if you'd like to set up your iMac to use the Internet, click Yes (or press Return) if you do.

3. If you already have an account with an Internet service provider (other than the EarthLink Network) or America Online (AOL), click Yes and skip to the section on "Using an existing Internet service provider (ISP)." If you don't have an Internet account yet (or do have one with EarthLink Network), click No and skip to the section on "Using a new Internet service provider (ISP)" later in this section.

Using an existing Internet service provider (ISP)

If you already have an Internet account, follow these steps to continue your setup in Internet Setup Assistant:

1. Gather your account information, such as domain name service (DNS) and IP addresses, configuration types, access numbers, and your username and password. If you're unsure of any of this information, call your ISP to obtain it.

2. Input your account information in Internet Setup Assistant.

When you finish, you should be ready to connect to the Internet. If it doesn't work, choose the Apple Menu⇨Control Panels⇨Internet and modify your information.

 If you have an EarthLink account, you can use the configuration software instead of Internet Setup Assistant. You can find it on Macintosh HD⇨Internet⇨Internet Applications⇨EarthLink Total Access⇨Registration & Utilities.

If you have an America Online account, you do not need to use Internet Setup Assistant. Instead, locate the America Online application in your Internet folder on the Macintosh HD and double-click it to open it. Follow the directions provided on the screen to set up the software for your existing America Online account.

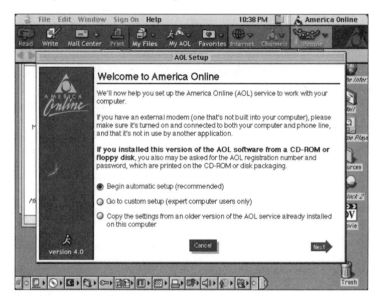

Using a new Internet service provider (ISP)

The EarthLink Network is an Internet service provider (ISP) that you can use for your Internet access. Your iMac comes with configuration software for EarthLink, making it a good choice for those who are new to the Internet. The first month with EarthLink is free of charge; monthly costs thereafter are about $20 (at the time of writing), and you may need to pay an hourly charge of about $5 to use their toll-free access number if no local number is available in your area. If you are interested in other options, check your phone book for local Internet service providers.

If you decide to go with EarthLink, follow these steps:

1. If you clicked No when asked if you already have an Internet account in Internet Setup Assistant, the EarthLink Registration & Utilities configuration software opens automatically for you. If you prefer to open this software directly, it is located at Macintosh HD⇨Internet⇨Internet Applications⇨EarthLink Total Access⇨Registration & Utilities.

2. Click the Setup button (unless you already have an EarthLink Network account, in which case you should click Retrieve).

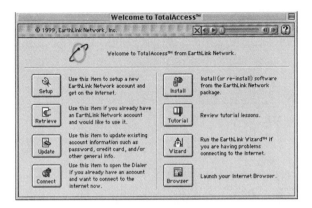

3. Enter your new username and password. Choose these carefully — your username becomes part of your e-mail address and your password becomes your first line of defense in protecting your account. Generally, you want a short and simple username and a long and complicated password. You should be able to easily remember both.

4. After you choose your username and password, click Next (or press Return).

5. Set up your phone (and modem) and select your service. Have your credit card handy because you need to provide payment information to establish your account.

When the setup process is complete, you can open Internet applications and be automatically connected to the Internet. You can also connect to the Internet using Remote Access (Apple Menu⇨ Control Panels⇨Remote Access). If you need to change your Internet configuration at any time, choose the Apple Menu⇨ Control Panels⇨Internet and modify as necessary.

If you've set up your new EarthLink account already but are having problems connecting to it, the culprit may simply be your local access number. To find a new local access number, follow these steps:

1. Open the EarthLink configuration software at Macintosh HD⇨ Internet⇨Internet Applications⇨EarthLink Total Access⇨ Registration & Utilities.

2. Click Update.

3. Click Phone.

4. Select a new local access number from the list. If you do not see a viable number, click the Update button to get the latest list. You may need to click Additional Settings to add or remove dialing instructions.

5. Click OK when done to update your Internet settings on your iMac.

Finding Information on the Internet

After you configure your iMac to connect to the Internet, you can use your iMac to tap into vast databases of information. The net effect is an immensely huge increase in your iMac's capabilities and usefulness. Understanding how and where to find this information isn't as easy, however. This section shows you how to access the World Wide Web using an ISP or AOL, and then how to find information on the Web using search engines and Sherlock 2.

Connecting to the World Wide Web

To connect to the World Wide Web, you need an Internet connection and a Web browser. The previous section covered Internet connection, and your iMac comes with three Web browsers.

To connect to the Web, double-click the Browse the Internet icon on your desktop. Assuming you already configured your Internet connection, this action should log you on to your Internet service provider and then open a Web browser window on your screen.

If you use AOL, the AOL software opens and waits for you to sign on. If you already signed on to AOL, a Web browser window is automatically displayed for you.

When your Web browser is open, you've established your connection to the Web. If this is your first connection to the Web using EarthLink, you need to type your username and password for configuration of your start page. If you do this, your Web browser displays a personalized start page for you when you initiate your connection to the Web. If you're using AOL, you see the AOL Web site initially — if you prefer to change this to another page, choose My AOL⇨Preferences⇨WWW and enter a new address for your home page.

If you prefer to use a different Web browser than the one that opens, follow these steps:

1. Choose the Apple menu⇨Control Panels⇨Internet.

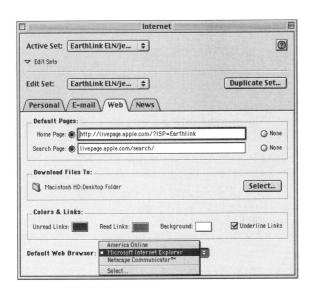

2. Click the Web tab.

3. Select your preferred Web browser from the drop-down menu at the bottom.

Many Internet connections, including EarthLink and America Online, automatically disconnect you within a few minutes if you are not actively using the Internet. If you are disconnected from EarthLink or a similar ISP, you can reconnect by choosing the Apple menu⇨Control Panels⇨Remote Access and clicking Connect. If you want to disconnect, simply visit the Remote Access Control panel and click Disconnect.

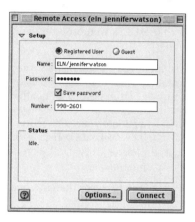

If you are disconnected from AOL, simply sign on again as you usually do.

Finding with search engines

Search engines are one way to find specific information on the Internet. To use a search engine, first establish your connection to the Web.

If you use the Internet Explorer Web browser (check the name at the far right of your menu bar), follow these steps:

1. Click the Search icon at the top of the browser window. This opens the search tab along the left side of the window.

2. Choose a search engine from the provider drop-down menu near the top of the search window. Several options are available and all have their pros and cons, though for the most part it is a personal choice. For your first foray, I recommend InfoSeek.

3. Type a word or phrase that describes what you're looking for into the text entry field. Don't be too generic (like **software** or **Mac**). Be sure you spell the word or phrase correctly, too.

4. Click the Search button next to the text entry field to begin your search.

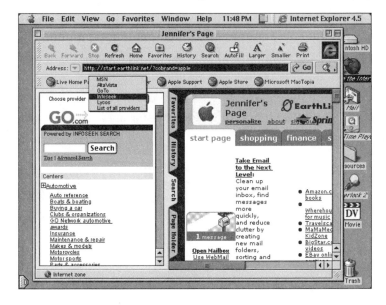

If you're using the America Online (AOL) Web browser, follow these steps:

1. Choose Find⇨Find it on the Web (the Find button in the toolbar near the top of the AOL window). This opens a window with AOL.COM Search.

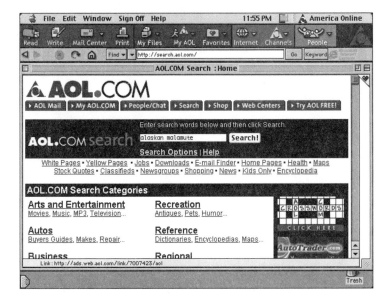

2. Type a word or phrase that describes what you're looking for into the text entry field.

3. Click the Search! button next to the text entry field to begin your search.

If you're using the Netscape Navigator browser, follow these steps:

1. Click the Search icon at the top of the browser window. This displays the Apple/Excite search page.

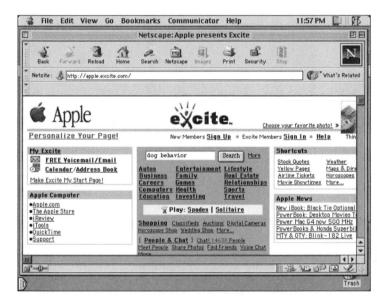

2. Type a word or phrase that describes what you're looking for into the text entry field.

3. Click the Search button next to the text entry field to begin your search.

After a few seconds of searching, your browser displays the search results. Results are generally listed in the order of relevancy and you probably need to scroll through your window to see them all. You can click on a blue hyperlink to go to a page. If none of the results seem right, look near the bottom of the page for a Next or More Results hyperlink to see more matches. If your search returned too many results, or not enough, try a different search using more specific or more general search words or phrases.

As you search the Web, you may notice that a string of characters beginning with http:// appears near the top of your Web browser. This is a page's address. You can go directly to a Web page if you know its address. For example, type **www.apple.com** (just the way it appears here) and press Return to go to Apple Computer's Web page.

If you don't find what you seek in your Web browser's default search page, try another page. If you're looking for something very specific, visit Lycos (`www.lycos.com`) and AltaVista (`www.altavista.com`) — both of these Web pages attempt to index everything on the Web, so you should get plenty of results. If you're looking for quality pages or categories of pages, try Yahoo! (`www.yahoo.com`), which prides itself on being a directory to the best of the Web. If you're looking for phone numbers, try Four11 (`www.four11.com`). Many more Web pages for finding other pages, people, and places exist — try searching for them in your Web browser.

Finding with Sherlock 2

You have another, potentially more powerful tool for finding information: Sherlock 2. You may know that Sherlock searches your hard drive for files, but it can also search the Internet for information. Note that Sherlock 2 is a new feature of Mac OS 9. Mac OS 8 offers an earlier version of Sherlock that can also search the Internet, but it is not as powerful. This section covers Sherlock 2.

To search the Internet with Sherlock 2, follow these steps:

1. Choose the Apple menu⇨Sherlock 2. Alternately, if you're using Microsoft Internet Explorer, click the magnifying glass button on the far right end of the browser window and select Open Apple Sherlock.

2. When Sherlock 2 opens, click the Globe button near the top of the window.

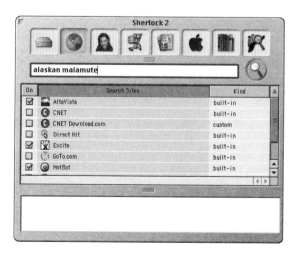

3. Type your word or phrase in the text entry field.

4. Check the pages you'd like to search from the list below the text entry field.

5. Click the magnifying glass icon to begin searching.

Assuming you are connected to the Internet, Sherlock takes a few seconds to search and displays matches as it finds them. Results are organized in order of relevancy, though you can change that by clicking a column heading to re-sort the list by name or site.

Simply double-click a match to view the page in your Web browser.

The other buttons along the top of Sherlock 2 represent different search channels you can use to narrow your search. Here's the skinny on each:

🖙 The woman icon leads to the People Channel, where you can search sites for information about individuals.

🖙 The shopping cart icon enables you to search for books, music, videos, and items for sale in auctions.

🖙 The newspaper icon offers searches in news-related Web sites like CNN, ESPN, and Motley Fool.

🖙 The Apple icon lets you search Apple's products guide, Tech Info Library, and Apple.com.

🖙 The Books icon allows you to search a dictionary, thesaurus, and encyclopedia.

If you'd like to create your own channel in Sherlock 2, see the next section.

For best results, keep your Sherlock search plug-ins up-to-date by visiting the Sherlock plug-in download site at `www.apple.com/sherlock/plugins.html`.

Making custom channels in Sherlock 2

If you find yourself searching specific sites in Sherlock 2 with frequency, you may prefer to create your own custom channel. Here's how to do it:

1. Open Sherlock 2.

2. Choose Channels⇨New Channel.

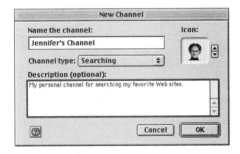

3. Type an appropriate name for the new channel.

4. Select an appropriate icon for the new channel using the up and down arrows.

5. Choose an appropriate channel type from the drop-down menu.

6. Type an appropriate description for the new channel, if desired.

7. Click OK.

8. When you return to the main Sherlock 2 window, resize the window by clicking-and-dragging the three diagonal lines in the lower-right corner of the window. Make the window wider until you can see your new channel icon appear at the end of the row of icons at the top. Click your channel icon to display it.

9. Click other channel icons that contain the Web sites you'd like to add to your new channel.

10. To add a site to your channel, hold down the Option key and click-and-drag a search site from an existing channel to your new channel icon. If you don't hold down the Option key, you move the search site rather than make a new copy of it. Alternately, you may visit the Sherlock Plug-Ins Web site (www.apple.com/sherlock/plugins.html), download a plug-in for a site you'd like to add to your channel, and click-and-drag it to your channel in Sherlock 2.

To edit your channel later, select your channel in Sherlock, choose Channels⇨Edit Channel, and make the necessary changes. You can delete any channels you create by selecting the channel and then choose Channels⇨Delete Channel.

Navigating the World Wide Web

As you move to a new page on the Web, your Web browser refreshes your window to display the new page content. Tools near the top of your Web browser window enable you to navigate backward and forward through the pages, as well as perform other tasks. Here's what each of the navigational buttons do:

✔ To return to a page you previously visited, click the Back button at the top of your screen (a left arrow).

✔ To move forward again, click the Forward button (a right arrow).

✔ To cancel the display of a Web page, click the Stop button (a circle with an *X* in it).

✔ To redraw the page in the window, click the Refresh or Reload button (circular arrow).

✔ To return to your home (first) page, click the Home button (it usually looks like a small house).

Sending and Receiving E-mail

Your iMac can send and receive *e-mail* (electronic mail) whether you use an ISP or America Online, though the process differs considerably. This section looks at each process individually.

Using e-mail on America Online

To read e-mail on America Online, follow these steps:

1. Open your AOL application and sign on to the service.

2. If you hear "You've got mail!" upon sign on, click the mailbox icon to display your list of mail.

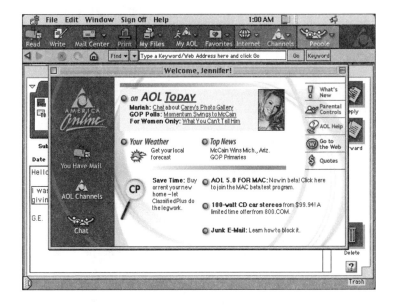

3. In the resulting list of e-mail, double-click an e-mail name to view it.

4. To see new e-mail that has arrived since you clicked on your mailbox icon, press ⌘+R or choose Mail Center⇨Read Mail.

To send a response to an e-mail message, follow these steps:

1. Click Reply in the e-mail window.

Highlight text you'd like from the e-mail you received before you click Reply to include that text in your e-mail response. This is helpful when you are responding to a question.

2. Type your message in the new window that appears.

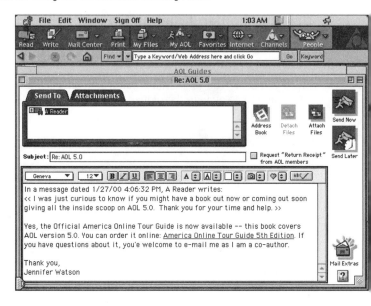

3. Click Send. AOL confirms that your e-mail was sent.

To send a new e-mail message, follow these steps:

1. Click the Write icon on the toolbar at the top of the screen.

2. Type your recipient's e-mail address. If you are unsure of their address, use the people channel search in Sherlock 2 to search for it, or choose People⇨Search AOL Member Directory in AOL (if you're looking for AOL members).

3. Type a subject line.

4. Type your message.

5. Click Send. AOL confirms that your e-mail was sent.

To learn more about using AOL e-mail, click the Mail Center icon on the toolbar and choose Mail Center. You can also check out an entire book on this subject, titled *AOL E-Mail* by yours truly and published by MIS Press. Look for it wherever you found this book!

Using Netscape Communicator

If you connect to the Internet through an ISP like EarthLink, you can use Netscape Communicator to access your e-mail. Here's how:

1. Open Netscape Communicator (Macintosh HD⇨Internet⇨ Netscape Communicator). If this is your first time launching Netscape Communicator, you need to create a profile — follow the directions on-screen.

2. Click the Inbox icon on the floating component bar. Alternately, choose Communicator⇨Messenger to view your inbox.

3. In the resulting list of e-mail, single-click an e-mail name to view it.

4. To see new e-mail that has arrived since you opened Netscape Communicator, click Get Msg in the toolbar.

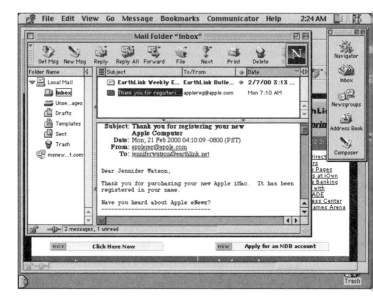

To reply to an e-mail in Netscape Communicator, follow these steps:

1. Click the Reply button on the toolbar at the top of the Inbox window.

2. Type your message. Note that Netscape Communicator automatically inserts a copy of the original e-mail message.

3. Click Send. Your message window closes after the e-mail is sent.

To send a new e-mail message in Netscape Communicator, follow these steps:

1. Click the New Msg button in the toolbar of the Inbox window.

2. Type your recipient's e-mail address. If you are unsure of their address, use the people channel search in Sherlock 2 to search for it.

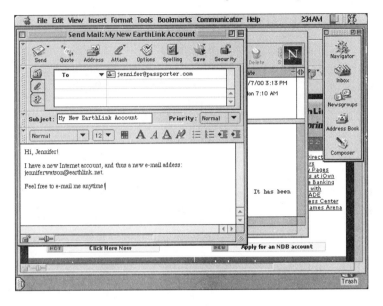

3. Type a subject line.

4. Type your message.

5. Click Send. Your message window closes after the e-mail is sent.

To learn more about sending and receiving e-mail through Netscape Communicator, choose Help⇨Help and click Using E-Mail in the resulting window.

Using Outlook Express

Your iMac comes with Outlook Express, which is a dedicated e-mail program. Outlook Express may be used for e-mail through an ISP, but not for e-mail on AOL. If you used Internet Setup Assistant to connect to the Internet, you're probably set up to use Outlook Express already. Here's how to use it:

1. Double-click the Mail alias on your desktop — Outlook Express opens if your Internet settings are configured to do so. If Outlook Express doesn't open, choose the Apple Menu⇨ Control Panels⇨Internet, click the E-mail tab, and choose Outlook Express from the drop-down menu at the bottom.

2. Opening Outlook initiates an e-mail check — if any new e-mail is found, Outlook Express displays it in bold in your Inbox. Click once on a message to view it in the bottom half of the window.

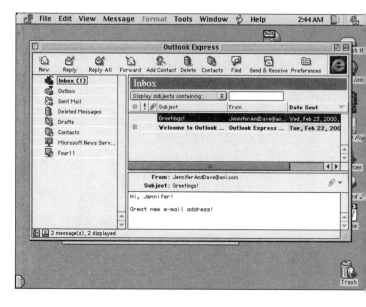

3. To see if any new e-mail has arrived since you opened Outlook
Express, press ⌘+Shift+M or choose Tools➪Send & Receive➪
Receive All.

To reply to an e-mail message in Outlook Express, follow these
steps:

1. Click the Reply button at the top of a message window.

2. Type your own message. Note that Outlook Express automatically includes a copy of the text that appeared in the original
e-mail.

3. Click Send Now. Outlook Express closes your mail message
window and displays a status bar to show you the progress of
your e-mail as it is sent.

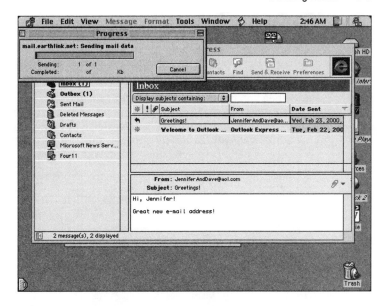

To send a new e-mail message in Outlook Express, follow these steps:

1. Click the New button in the toolbar.

2. Type your recipient's e-mail address. If you are unsure of their address, use the people channel search in Sherlock 2 to search for it.

3. Type a subject line.

4. Type your message.

5. Click Send Now. Outlook Express closes your mail message window and displays a status bar to show you the progress of your e-mail as it is sent.

For more help using Outlook Express, choose Outlook Express Help from the Help menu.

Sending Faxes

While unrelated to the Internet, faxing is another way to connect your iMac to the outside world. Your iMac comes with the FAXstf software, which enables you to send and receive faxes.

Configuring FAXstf

To configure FAXstf, follow these steps:

1. Open the Fax Browser application (Macintosh HD⇨ Applications⇨FAXstf⇨Fax Browser).

2. When you're prompted to register, I recommend you elect to register later after you set up your fax software. (Don't forget to register later, however!) You may also be shown a list of additional features and functions available if you upgrade your copy of FAXstf — click Done to dismiss it for now.

3. After the Fax Browser window appears, choose Edit⇨Settings.

4. Click the Cover Page icon to view its settings.

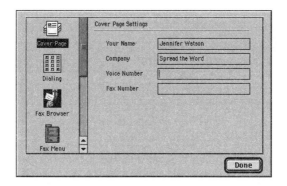

5. Type your name, company/school/organization name, voice number, and fax number. This information will be displayed on outgoing faxes, so be sure to type in only what you want others to see.

6. Click Done to save your changes to the settings.

To set up your fax address book, follow these steps:

1. Choose Windows⇨Fax Numbers (or click the phone book icon in the Fax Browser window).

2. Choose Action⇨New Contact (or click the New Contact button). A blank line appears in the chart.

3. Type your contact's information, pressing Tab to move to the next column. Be sure to include at least a name and a fax number. Repeat as necessary. If someone has two fax numbers, use the Duplicate feature — you need to type only the fax number in the duplicate line.

4. When you finish, click Lock Phonebook to protect your data (and allow the numbers to be selected when faxing later).

If you forget to click Lock Phonebook, closing the window automatically locks it for you. You need to manually unlock and lock the Phonebook if you intend to keep it open on your screen, however — the phonebook needs to be locked before the fax software can use it.

Creating a cover page

Cover pages introduce your fax to your recipient(s) and communicate any essential information, such as fax length or comments. FAXstf lets you create up to ten different cover pages to use when sending faxes. Here's how to create a cover page:

1. Choose Edit⇨Edit Cover Pages to see your cover page options.

2. To create a new cover page, choose Empty Cover Page from the drop-down menu.

3. Type a name for your new cover page.

4. Click Edit Labels Text to change the cover page font and rename the labels used on it if you wish.

5. If you want to change the layout of the cover page, click-and-drag the elements represented in the window as desired.

6. Click OK to save changes to your cover page.

Receiving a fax

To set up your fax software to receive a fax, follow these steps:

1. Choose Edit⇨Settings, click the Fax Modem icon, and change your Answer On setting from Never to One Ring (if you have a dedicated modem line) or Two to Three Rings (if you use your line for voice, too). Don't go higher than five rings, however, because some fax machines give up after five or six rings. Click Done.

2. When your phone line rings, the FAXstf software answers your phone with a standard fax tone. If the incoming call is indeed a fax, the software begins receiving it and displays the FaxStatus window during the transmission.

If you wish, you can stop the transmission by clicking the Stop button in the FaxStatus window. Alternately, you can press ⌘+. (period).

3. After you successfully receive the fax transmission, you hear a ring (sounds like a phone) and a blinking icon appears over the Apple menu to indicate you have a new fax. All incoming fax transmissions are archived in the FAX In folder in your Fax Browser. To view your new fax, switch to your Fax Browser, click Fax In, and double-click your most recent fax.

You can scroll through the fax like you would a document. Use the magnifying glass button in the tool palette to zoom in — press and hold the Option key while clicking to zoom out. Other buttons on the tool palette let you change views and rotate the fax. Use the menu items under the Action menu to see your fax in various ways, including as a continuous "roll" of paper (like the old fashioned fax machines) or regular page breaks. Select Antialiased for the best quality display, or Fast for a rougher view. If you need a hard copy of the fax, you can print it as you would any other document (***see also*** Part VI for more information on printing).

Setting up your fax software to answer your phone can be a problem if you share the same line with voice calls. Ideally, you should only allow the fax software to answer the phone when you expect to receive a fax. Otherwise, your iMac attempts to answer all voice calls with fax tones, which is annoying to both you and your caller.

Sending a fax

Your fax software enables you to send faxes two ways. If you just
want to dash off a fast fax, the Fax Browser provides a QuickNote
feature that lets you send a fax up to 255 characters in length (***see
also*** "Sending a QuickNote fax" later in this part). If, on the other
hand, you want to send a longer fax, or one that is formatted or
includes graphics, you can send a fax directly from the application
you composed it in (such as AppleWorks). Here's how to do it:

1. Compose your fax document in another application (such as
AppleWorks), keeping in mind that your font should be no
smaller than 12 point for legibility. (Refer to Part V for more
information on other applications.)

2. Choose the Apple menu⇨Chooser and click the FaxPrint icon.
Close the window.

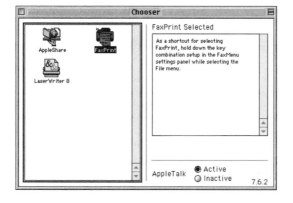

3. Return to your application and choose File⇨Fax.

4. Select the resolution and page span.

5. If you added the necessary information to your Phonebook,
you should also see fax numbers in the list box on the left. (***See
also*** "Configuring FAXstf" to learn how to add addresses.) To
address your fax, click-and-drag a number from the left box to
the right box. You can add as many destinations as you like. If
your recipient isn't in your phone book, press ⌘+N to add a
temporary address.

6. Click Options to schedule your fax for later and/or to select a
cover page.

7. When ready, click Send to initiate the faxing process. The
software displays a status bar to keep you informed of the
progress.

Sending a QuickNote fax

QuickNote faxes are those you send from within the fax software. Here's how to do it:

1. Open the Fax Browser and choose File⇨Send a QuickNote (or press ⌘+K).

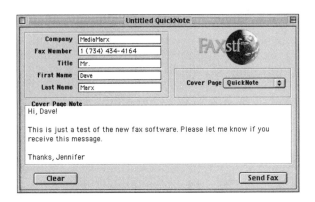

2. Enter your contact information. If you've already added the contact information for your fax recipient to your Phonebook, you can click-and-drag it from the Phonebook to the QuickNote window.

3. Type your "quick" note. You may have up to 255 characters in your note.

4. Select a cover page from the drop-down menu, if you wish.

5. Click Send Fax to instantly send the fax.

After you send a QuickNote fax, your modem dials your recipient's fax number and initiates the fax transmission. When complete, a dialog box informs you that your fax was sent successfully. FAXstf files a copy of the fax you sent in the FAX Archive section should you need to check it later.

Part V

Applying Your iMac

You've got this great iMac. Now what are you going to do with it? Your options are virtually endless. You could write a letter . . . or a book. Why not try creating a database of addresses or research notes? Or get even more ambitious — prepare a spreadsheet of household bills or corporate financials? Your iMac can take you from the simplest task to the most complex.

Where to begin? First, learn the basics of installing and opening applications. Next, explore one of the most versatile applications on your iMac: AppleWorks. Learn how to manipulate text in the word processor, create records and fields in the database, and calculate numbers in the spreadsheet.

In this part . . .

Applications

Applications are software programs that you can install and run on your iMac. Most applications have specific purposes, such as displaying graphics or managing money. You already have a good collection of applications on your iMac — some of which may or may not need to be installed — but you can also find more applications on the Internet and in computer stores. If you have a new application, use this part to learn how to install it, open it, register it, and quit it.

Installing applications

Your iMac comes with many applications preinstalled. Even so, a few need to be installed before you can use them, such as Adobe PageMill, World Book Encyclopedia, and Kid Pix (which comes with newer iMacs). Most software that you need to install comes on CD-ROM, as the previously mentioned applications do. (Check the CD wallet that came with your iMac.) To install new software, follow these steps:

1. Quit all open applications. Installations usually go more smoothly if no other applications are running while you're installing. If you're not sure how to exit applications, see "Quitting applications" later in this section.

2. Locate and load the CD-ROM that holds the software you want to install. Alternately, you may be able to download software from the Internet.

3. Double-click the Installer icon. This icon may alternately be labeled either Install or Begin Here.

4. Follow the on-screen directions, which differ from program to program, and answer any questions necessary.

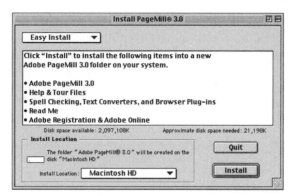

5. When prompted, select a location for your new software. Usually an Install Location drop-down menu is available near the bottom of the main installation screen. To choose a specific folder on a hard drive, choose Install Location⇨Select Folder, select a folder in the dialog box, and click Select. The Applications folder is appropriate for new software, though you could create a new folder with the New Folder button, too.

6. Click Install to begin transferring the software files to your iMac. If you need to quit any open applications, you get the opportunity to do so before continuing. A status thermometer keeps you up-to-date on the progress.

7. Click Restart if you're prompted to restart your iMac after installation. Restarting your iMac after installing new software is a good idea even if it isn't required.

After successfully installing the new application and returning to your desktop, you should see an open window containing your new application. Double-click the main application icon to run it.

Some applications (such as the World Book Encyclopedia) copy only a few files to your hard drive — you need to insert the disc every time you want to run the application. Other applications (such as Adobe PageMill) are entirely copied to your hard drive — you may never use the disc again unless a problem occurs and you have to reinstall the application. Still others (like Quicken Deluxe and iMovie) have extra goodies on the CD-ROM that aren't copied to your hard drive, but also aren't crucial to running the application.

Opening applications

Use one of these techniques to open an application:

✔ Double-click the application file on the desktop. Application file icons usually bear the name of the application itself and have logos that represent what the application does. The SimpleText application (Macintosh HD⇨Applications⇨SimpleText) is a good example.

✔ Double-click a file icon to open it *and* the application that created it (or can read it). Document icons often look like pieces of paper or newspapers, sometimes with a "corner" turned down. The iMac Read Me and iMovie Read Me files (in Macintosh HD) are examples of documents.

✔ Double-click an alias to open the original application or file. *Aliases* are shortcuts to other files; unless the alias goes to a folder, you're probably opening an application. The Browse the Internet alias on your desktop is a good example of an alias that opens an application.

✔ Select an icon and choose File⇨Open. Alternately, you can control+click an icon and choose Open from the contextual menu.

✔ Click-and-drag a document icon on top of the application icon that created it.

✔ Choose the application from the Apple menu if a shortcut to it exists or if the application appears in the Recent Applications submenu. Choosing files from the Recent Documents submenu also opens that application if it isn't already open.

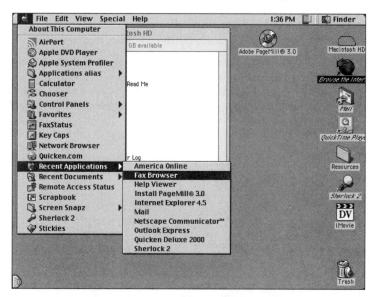

 Occasionally, when you double-click a file icon, your iMac informs you that it could not find the application program that created the document. If this happens, the same window that informed you of this situation also presents a list of applications that may be able to open the file instead. You may double-click one of these applications and try to open your file in it.

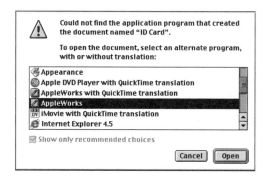

Opening files within applications

After an application is open, you can open associated files within it. Here's how to do just that:

1. Open the application.

2. Choose File⇨Open.

3. Locate and select the file you want to open.

   Your iMac displays a list of files, usually those associated with the running application. You can scroll through this list using the up and down arrows. Double-click a folder in the list to see its contents. Use the drop-down menu near the top of the window to move up one or more folders. The Desktop button on the right side quickly takes you to the top level of your hard drive. Some applications offer previews of documents to help you find the one you're seeking, while others allow you to see only files of certain types to let you weed out the irrelevant information.

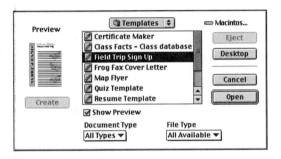

4. Open the file by either clicking Open or double-clicking the file-name in the list.

Registering applications

Some applications, such as AppleWorks, ask you for information the first time you open them. You may be asked to type your name, your company's name, and/or your serial number or registration code. Serial numbers and registration codes are unique and are generally used to discourage copying and sharing programs with those who haven't purchased them. If you're looking for your application's serial number or registration code, try these nooks and crannies:

✔ Check your software's documentation.

✔ Check the envelope of the software disc. (The World Book Encyclopedia CD-Key number is on its envelope in the disc wallet that came with your iMac.)

✔ Check the papers that came with your iMac. (A registration number and password for new America Online accounts is on a sheet in your Accessory Kit.)

AppleWorks may or may not need a serial number. Try registering without it. If it insists on having a serial number, use your computer's serial number. Look for your computer's serial number on a label inside your access panel (on the right side of your iMac) or on the underside of your iMac (under the foot rest).

Setting application preferences

Virtually all applications have *preferences,* a set of options you can set to optimize the application for your needs. To set an application's preferences, follow these steps:

1. Open an application.

2. Choose Edit⇨Preferences. Alternately, you may find the preferences under the File menu or by another name, such as Settings, Options, or Customize.

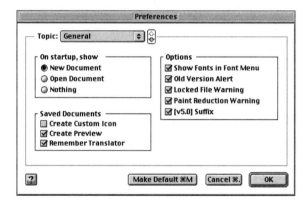

3. Set your options as desired. Look for additional option categories under icons or drop-down menus.

4. Click OK or Set Preferences to save your settings. Some preferences may not take place until you quit and reopen the application.

Switching between applications

Use one of these techniques to switch between open applications on your iMac:

✔ Select the window of the application you want to switch to (assuming you can see the window in the background).

✔ Select the Application menu on the far right of your menu bar and select the application to which you want to switch.

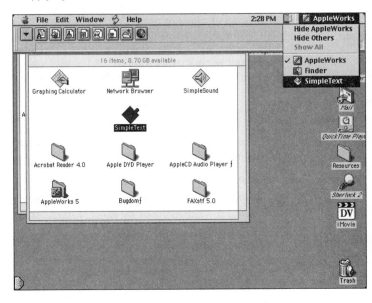

🖝 Press ⌘+Tab to cycle to another open application. Repeat until you come to the open application you want.

Quitting applications

To *quit,* or close, an application, follow these steps:

1. Save any work (open files) you have open by choosing File⇨Save (or pressing ⌘+S).

2. Choose File⇨Quit. Alternately, press ⌘+Q.

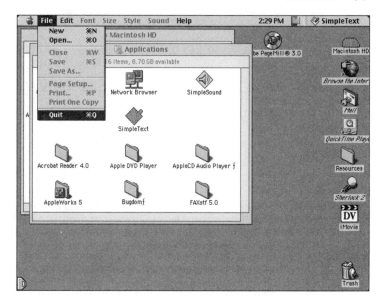

3. If you are asked to make sure you want to quit, confirm it by clicking OK or Quit.

Databases

A *database* is an organized system for saving, searching, sorting, and arranging information. Your iMac can store information in a computer database using AppleWorks.

Creating a database

To create a new database, follow these steps:

1. Open AppleWorks.

2. When prompted to create a new document, choose Database from the list on the left and click OK. If AppleWorks is already open, choose File⇨New or click the Database button in the toolbar (the one with the little Rolodex in front of a document).

3. In the resulting Define Database Fields window, type the name of the first field in your database. A *field* is where you enter capsules of information, such as a first name or a phone number. For example, if you were creating a new database of addresses, your first field may be called First Name.

```
┌─────────────────────────────────────────────────────────────┐
│                   Define Database Fields                       │
├─────────────────────────────────────────────────────────────┤
│   Field Name:                      Field Type:                 │
│  ┌─────────────────────────────────────────────────────┐ ▲   │
│  │                                                       │     │
│  │                                                       │     │
│  │                                                       │     │
│  │                                                       │     │
│  │                                                       │ ▲   │
│  └─────────────────────────────────────────────────────┘ ▼   │
│                                                                │
│   Field Name: │First Name│         Field Type: │Text ▼│       │
│  ┌────────────┐  ┌──────────┐  ┌──────────┐  ┌───────────┐    │
│  │ Create ⌘R  │  │Modify ⌘M │  │Delete ⌘E │  │Options...⌘O│   │
│  └────────────┘  └──────────┘  └──────────┘  └───────────┘    │
│  ┌?┐ Type a field name and click Create, or select a field,    │
│  └─┘ make changes, and     ┌──────────┐                        │
│      then click Modify.    │ Done ⌘D  │                        │
│                            └──────────┘                        │
└─────────────────────────────────────────────────────────────┘
```

4. Choose from the Field Type drop-down menu to the right of
the Field Name box. Text is the most appropriate field for fields
that contain text, but you can also choose from a variety of
other types, such as number, date, time, and so on.

5. Click Create to add the field to your database.

6. Repeat Steps 3 through 5 until you've added all necessary
fields.

7. Click Done when finished adding fields. You can add fields
later, if you want.

8. Choose File➪Save to save your new database.

 The Options button in the Define Database Fields dialog box lets you
set preferences for individual fields. For example, the Cannot Be
Empty option means that there must always be data in a particular
field. The Must Be Unique field means that data entered cannot
match already existing data in the database. The Default Text field
lets you designate text to be automatically inserted in your database.

Entering data

A database is only a shell until you enter data into it. Data is stored
in *fields,* and sets of data are stored in *records.* For example, if you
have a database of 100 addresses, you would store each name in
the Name field, each address in the Address field, each phone
number in the Number field, and so on. You wouldn't put all 100
names in a single Name field, however; instead, you'd create a new
record for each name. Thus, if you have 100 addresses, you would
have 100 records.

To create a new record in a database, choose Edit➪New Record.
Alternately, you can press ⌘+R or click the Create Record button
on the toolbar (a form with an arrow beside it). This inserts a new
record below the first record (or the record you're currently at).

You can enter information into the new record fields the same way you did with the first record. To begin entering data in a database record, follow these steps:

1. Open or create a database in AppleWorks.

2. Position your pointer in the first field at the top of the window and click. The outline of the field box changes from gray to black and the insertion point appears in the box. If you don't see the field box or insertion point, press the Tab key once.

3. Type your information.

4. Press Tab to move to the next field.

5. Continue through the fields, adding information to each one as you go. If you don't have information for a field, you may leave it empty if you didn't set the Cannot Be Empty option for it.

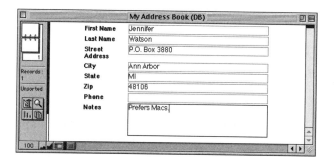

6. Press ⌘+R to create a new record and repeat Steps 2 through 5 as necessary.

Use the diagram of a Rolodex on the left side of the database window to move between records. To go directly to a specific record, click the number below the Rolodex, type in a new number, and press Return. You can also press ⌘+G to move to a particular record.

Generating a list of records

When data is in a database, you can display it record by record (cumbersome) or as a list (convenient). To generate a list of records, follow these steps:

1. Open a database in AppleWorks.

2. Choose Layout➪List or press ⌘+Shift+L.

	First Name	Last Name	Stree	City	Stat	Zip	P	Notes
	Jennifer	Watson	P.O.	Ann Arbor	MI	48106		Prefers Macs.
	Kim	Larner						Has a Mac Quadra.
	Carolyn	Tody			MI			Has a Mac Performa.

My Address Book (DB)

AppleWorks displays your data in neat little columns and rows. If a column is too narrow or too wide, click-and-drag the line between two of the column headings to a new location. This works for row depth, too. To rearrange the columns themselves, click-and-drag the column headings left or right.

Sorting records

To sort — or arrange — your records according to certain criteria, follow these steps:

1. Choose Organize⇨Sort Records or press ⌘+J.

2. Select the field you want to sort by in the list on the left.

3. Click the Move button.

4. If you have a lot of records in your database with the same information, repeat Steps 2 and 3 to add a second field to the Sort Order list for further alphabetic sorting.

5. Click OK to being sorting.

Spreadsheets

Spreadsheets are a specialized kind of database that can store and calculate numbers quickly and automatically. Common uses for spreadsheets include accounting, budgeting, financial analyzing, and so on. Sure, you can use a common calculator to do these things, but that is neither convenient nor as accurate. After you set up a spreadsheet, you can change one number and — poof — every subtotal, total, and formula is automatically updated. Spreadsheets also offer the highly readable row-and-column layout, much like traditional ledgers.

Creating a spreadsheet

To create a new spreadsheet in AppleWorks, open AppleWorks and choose Spreadsheet when prompted to open a new document. If AppleWorks is already running, choose File⇨New or click the Spreadsheet button in the toolbar (the one with a ledger in front of a document).

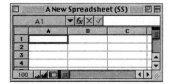

Spreadsheets are organized along a grid. Columns with alphabetic headings appear across the top, and rows with numeric headings appear down the left side. The columns and rows form small boxes, called *cells,* which are identified by the column letter and row number. For example, the box in column A and row 1 is cell A1.

Entering data

To enter data into a spreadsheet, follow these steps:

1. Open or create a spreadsheet in AppleWorks.

2. Position your pointer in a cell and select it.

3. Type your data. The information goes into the entry field at the top of the spreadsheet rather than directly into the cell.

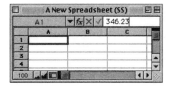

4. Press the Return key. Alternately, you can click the green check mark near the top of the spreadsheet or select another cell.

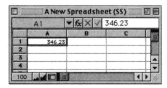

When a cell contains more information than it can display in its column, the spreadsheet displays the information in the adjacent cells (assuming the adjacent cells are empty). If you select an adjacent cell with runover information, the entry field at the top of the spreadsheet is blank, indicating that the cell is empty. Trace the stream of information to the left to find the actual cell. To increase

the depth of the column, position your pointer between two
column headings and click-and-drag to the left or right. Clicking
and dragging works for increasing row width, too.

Functions and calculations

One of the most useful parts of a spreadsheet is its capability to
perform complicated calculations. You can set up your spreadsheet
to do this by adding a formula to a cell. Follow these steps to do
just that:

1. Open or create a spreadsheet in AppleWorks.

2. Select the cell in which you would like to display the results of
a function or calculation. For example, single-click in cell A4.

3. Choose Edit⇨Paste Function.

4. Select a function from the resulting list and click OK. For example, you could choose the SUM function to add several numbers
together. If you're not sure of the meaning of each function in
the list, click the question-mark (?) button for assistance.

AppleWorks inserts the formula into the entry field at the top
of the spreadsheet.

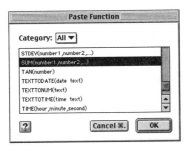

5. Select and delete everything in between the parentheses in
your formula — these are the *formula arguments* and you need
to specify them for your particular purposes. Formula arguments are the specific instructions for a calculation.

6. With your insertion point between the two parentheses in your
formula, click the first cell that you want to add to your formula. AppleWorks adds the cell name (A1, for example) to your
formula.

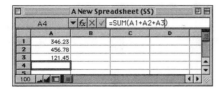

7. Continue clicking each cell that you want added to your formula. Alternately, you can click-and-drag a range of cells. For example, click-and-drag A1 through A3.

8. When finished, press the Return key. AppleWorks adds the amounts in the selected cells and displays the total in the formula cell. If you followed along in the example, your calculation would now add cells A1 + A2 + A3, displaying the total in cell A4.

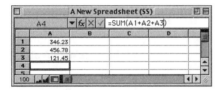

AppleWorks has a lot of ready-made formulas, but they can't anticipate everything you need to do. For example, to calculate an item's tax, you may want to create a formula that subtracts the discount from the list price and then calculate the tax from that price. To create a custom formula, follow these steps:

1. Select the cell to receive the formula.

2. Type an equal sign (=) in the entry field. The equal sign is the start of a formula in AppleWorks.

3. Click the first cell for your formula (the selling price cell, for example), type a minus sign (-), and click the second cell (the discount, for example). This tells AppleWorks to subtract the second cell from the first cell.

4. Put parentheses around the two cell names in the formula, like this: (B1-B2).

5. Position your insertion point at the end of your formula and type an asterisk (*). This tells AppleWorks to multiply the amount in parentheses by the amount that follows.

6. Click the third cell (tax percentage, for example) to place it in the formula.

	A New Spreadsheet (SS)			
B4	▼ *fx* × √	=(B1–B2)*B3		
	A	**B**	**C**	**D**
1	346.23	19.95	<-- list price	
2	456.78	2	<-- discount	
3	121.45	0.06	<-- tax rate	
4		1.077	<-- actual tax	
5				
6				

7. Press Return to save your formula.

Word Processing

Word processing is one of the most basic and useful tasks you can perform on your iMac. *Word processing* is really just a fancy phrase for creating things like letters and reports. Your iMac comes with a full-featured word processing application — AppleWorks.

Creating a new document

Some applications automatically create a new document for you when first opened. For example, Adobe PageMill creates a new, untitled document by default.

Other applications ask if you want to create a new document. In AppleWorks, an example of an application that prompts, you must also select the type of document you want to create (word processing, drawing, painting, spreadsheet, database, or communications).

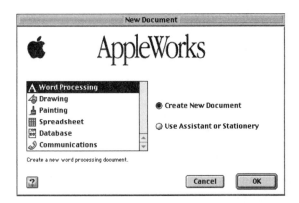

If an application does not prompt you to create a new document, follow these steps:

1. Choose File⇨New. If the New menu item is actually a submenu, select New Document or New Page.

2. If you are prompted to give your new document a title, type a descriptive name. You can rename the file later, if necessary.

3. Click New or Create, if necessary, to complete the process.

Alternately, you may be able to click a button in an application's toolbar to create a document. For example, the six icons on the far left of the AppleWorks toolbar enable you to create new documents of various types.

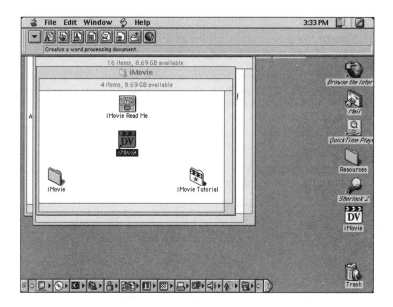

Editing text

You can edit text in a word processor (and most other applications) by using a set of common tools. Most of these edit tools are in your Edit menu, though many also appear in the AppleWorks toolbar. Here are the major editing techniques in alphabetical order:

✔ **Clear:** Removes and discards text. To use, select text and choose Edit⇨Clear.

✔ **Copy:** Records text for later. To use, select text and choose Edit⇨Copy (or press ⌘+C). *Note:* If you want to retain the copied text, you must paste it before copying or cutting more text.

✔ **Cut:** Removes text and records a copy for later. To use, select text and choose Edit⇨Cut (or press ⌘+X). If you want to retain the cut text, you must paste it before copying or cutting more text.

✔ **Paste:** Places the text last copied or cut. To use, position the pointer where you want the text to appear and choose Edit⇨Paste (or press ⌘+V).

✔ **Select All:** Selects all the text in a document for editing. To use, choose Edit⇨Select All (or press ⌘+A). Click anywhere in the window to deselect the text.

Fonts and formatting

Fonts and formatting are available in most word processing programs, including AppleWorks and SimpleText. To apply a font or format to a document before you begin typing, make the appropriate selections from the application's Font and/or Style menus. To apply a font or formatting to a section of text, you must first select the text. To select text, follow these steps:

1. Position your pointer, which looks like an *I* during word processing, at the start of the section you want to select.

2. Click-and-drag your pointer to the end of the section. The text is *highlighted* as you select it (the screen behind it turns black or another color).

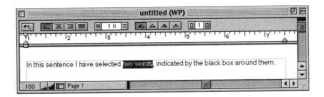

 To select an entire word, position your pointer directly over it and double-click. To select an entire line, position your pointer over it and triple-click. Note that in AppleWorks, doing so selects the line as it appears on the screen, not necessarily a full sentence. To select an entire paragraph, position your pointer over the paragraph and quadruple-click. To select all text in a document, press ⌘+A.

When text is selected (highlighted), you can choose a new font or style from the appropriately named menus in your application.

You don't have to choose a font before typing in a new document. A default font is used if you don't specifically choose another. You can change the default font in AppleWorks by choosing Edit⇨Preferences.

Saving your work

Saving any work you do in applications is essential. While some applications automatically save your work, most do not and you must manually save in order to avoid losing work. To save a file, follow these steps:

1. Choose File⇨Save.

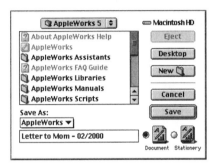

2. Select a location for your file in the window that appears. If you want to create a new folder for your document, click New, type a folder name, and click Create.

3. Type an appropriate name for your document. Your filename can be as long as 31 characters, but it must be different from other names in the folder to which you want to save it.

If you try to save a file with the same name as another file in that location, you are asked if you want to replace it. Be careful that you do not replace a file unless you intend to do so. You cannot retrieve a file if it is replaced.

Typing with the keyboard

You type on your keyboard to produce text — characters, numbers, symbols — in your word processing application. Your keyboard is divided into two main groups of keys. The largest group of keys is where you do almost all your typing, especially in a word processor. The letter and number keys are in the center, with special function keys like ⌘, Shift, and so on around the outside. The smaller group of keys on the right is the number pad and is laid out the same way as the keys on a calculator.

In addition to letters, numbers, and symbols, your keyboard has several special keys that you use on your iMac:

✔ Press the Tab key to shift the insert point across the page in preset increments.

✔ Press the Caps Lock key to turn all letters you type into capital letters. The Caps Lock key does not affect the numbers and punctuation marks. The key lights up when it is enabled; press it again to disable it.

✔ Press the Shift key to make capital letters. Hold it down and press a letter key at the same time to produce an uppercase character. You can also create symbols by holding down the Shift key and pressing a number key at the same time.

✔ Press and hold the Control, Option, and/or Command keys and another key to perform special operations and keyboard short-cuts. These functions are detailed throughout this book.

✔ Press the space bar (the long bar at the bottom of the keyboard without a word on it) to insert a blank space.

✔ Press the arrow keys (in the keyboard's lower-right corner) to move your insertion point up, down, left, and right.

✔ Press the Return key to insert a *hard return* when you want it, such as when you want to separate paragraphs.

✔ Press the Delete key to backspace over your text and erase it.

To begin typing, follow these steps:

1. Open an application and a document (or create a new document by choosing File⇨New).

2. Place your fingers on the keyboard in a natural position. Touch typists may note that the F and J keys have small bumps to provide you with a point of reference.

3. Begin typing when the document appears on your screen. Your text *insertion point* — the blinking vertical line — appears in the upper-left corner of a new document. This is where your text appears as you type.

Using templates

Applications, such as AppleWorks, often come with *templates,* which are preformatted documents that you can use as is or cus-tomize to your needs. For example, you may use a letterhead template to compose a new letter or memo, or a newsletter tem-plate to hold the articles you want to distribute around the office. The best thing about templates, aside from their convenience, is that when you open a template you're actually opening a copy of it. So you can make a letter or newsletter without changing the origi-nal template, and use that template again next week or next month.

To use templates in AppleWorks, follow these steps:

1. Open AppleWorks.

2. Choose File⇨Open, locate the AppleWorks Stationery folder, and open one of the Index files (such as the Letter and Letterhead Index or Memo Index).

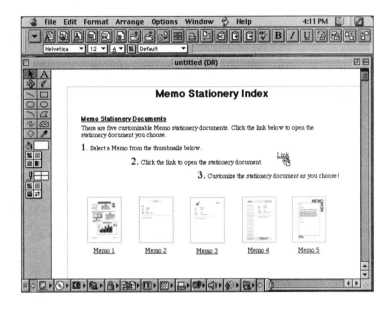

3. Click the blue, underlined link below a thumbnail to open and copy a stationery template. *Thumbnails* are small pictures that give you a sneak peek at the available template.

4. You may make changes to the document without modifying the template itself.

To create a new stationery file from an AppleWorks template, choose File⇨Save, select the Stationery option at the bottom of the resulting window, and save the file with an appropriate name. You can use this technique to create new templates from documents you create, too.

Printing Documents

Your iMac offers stunning graphics and crisp text on your screen, but what do you do when you want to share an image or document with someone else? Lugging your iMac around isn't exactly practical. The best solution is to print the image or document onto paper. To print, you must have a printer. The basic iMac system doesn't come with a printer, but you can purchase one separately or as part of an iMac package.

After you have a printer, read this part to learn how to connect your printer to your iMac, prepare it for printing, set up your document, and print your documents.

In this part . . .

Choosing a Printer

When you make the decision to purchase a printer for your iMac, you must consider two important requirements:

- The printer must be Mac-compatible.

- The printer must be able to connect to your iMac with Ethernet or USB.

If you purchase an Ethernet printer, you need either a special *crossover cable* or a *hub* — inquire when purchasing.

Beyond these requirements, you can choose from the following three general types of printers for your iMac:

- *Laser printers* are generally the most expensive. They use the same technology as photocopying machines and usually offer the highest print quality.

- *Inkjet printers* are the most affordable printers, and the quality is nearly as good as laser. Inkjet printers spray ink onto the paper and can usually print in color.

- *Dot-matrix printers* use an inked ribbon (like a typewriter). Dot-matrix printers aren't very common these days and you may have difficulties finding one for your iMac. If you need to print multi-part forms (carbon or carbonless), dot-matrix printers are still the only choice. Otherwise, dot-matrix printers are of lesser quality and slower speed than laser printers or inkjet printers.

Connecting your printer

To connect a printer to your iMac, follow these steps:

1. Open the box and locate the installation instructions. Read these carefully.

2. Remove the printer from the box and packing material.

3. Check the printer for tape that may have been used to secure the printer during shipping. Consult your installation instructions for information on how to remove this if you find it. Failure to remove the tape may cause serious problems.

4. Connect the printer to your iMac by following the instructions. Be sure to also plug it into a surge suppressor or wall outlet.

5. Locate the printer software and install the printer software on your iMac according to the instructions. If your printer software came on floppy disks, contact the manufacturer for a CD-ROM (unless you have an optional floppy disk drive).

6. Restart your iMac.

Selecting your printer in the Chooser

After you connect your printer and install the software, you must tell your iMac to use your printer. Here's how to do it:

1. Turn on your printer if it isn't already on.

2. Choose the Apple menu⇨Chooser.

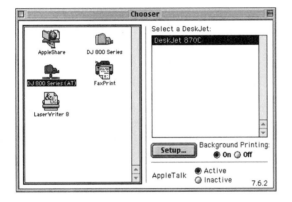

3. In the resulting window, single-click your printer's icon in the box on the left to select it. You should recognize your printer by name; if you don't, check your printer's documentation to see which icon to use. When you click the printer icon, the printer's name appears in the box on the right, indicating it is ready and waiting. If you see <Printer Port> and <Modem Port> appear instead, select <Printer Port>.

4. Close the Chooser and click OK in the resulting window.

Preparing to Print

Before you print a document, you need to prepare your printer and your document for printing. Without adequate preparation, your printed image quality may suffer significantly. Preparation takes only a few moments.

Servicing a printer

Printers — whether new or old — require occasional servicing for optimal printing. You should always service a printer after you connect a printer to your iMac or after your replace its toner cartridge, ink cartridge, or ink ribbon.

To service a laser printer, follow these steps:

1. Choose the Apple menu⇨Chooser.

2. Select your printer's icon in the box on the left.

3. Click the Create button, which should appear on the right. Your iMac displays a progress bar as it sets up your printer.

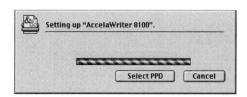

Setting up "AccelaWriter 8100".

Select PPD   Cancel

4. Your printer setup may offer different options. Refer to your printer's documentation for details. Other options may include selecting the *PPD file* (Printer Description File), displaying Printer Info (and updating it), and configuring your printer.

To service an inkjet printer, follow these steps:

1. Open an application that has the ability to print documents.

2. Choose File⇨Page Setup.

3. Click Service. If you do not have a button by this name, look for one called Utilities or Options. If you do not see any buttons by these names, choose File⇨Print and check there. Alternately, you can refer to your printer's documentation.

4. Choose your service options. Inkjet service options range from cleaning the ink cartridge before printing to aligning the ink cartridges. Performing each of these service functions before you use your printer is a good idea — they ensure you get the best possible image from your inkjet. Follow the directions onscreen to complete it.

Setting up a page

To make sure your document, page, or window is properly set up for printing, follow these steps:

1. Open the document you want to print in an application that supports printing, such as AppleWorks.

2. Choose File⇨Page Setup. The Page Setup window is often unique to your printer, but some elements remain the same, such as page size, layout, scale, and orientation. Here are some of the typical page setup options you may find:

- **Paper/Media Size:** Most Page Setup windows default to letter page size (8.5" x 11"), but you can often select other sizes (such as legal size) from the page size drop-down menu. Be sure your printer supports the paper size before you select it, however.

- **Media:** This option enables you to choose the kind of paper in your printer. Inkjet printers use this option to determine the proper amount of ink.

- **Orientation:** This option determines whether your document is printed in the default portrait (vertical) or landscape (horizontal) view.

- **Layout:** This option lets you print several pages of a document onto one piece of paper, assuming your document is small enough.

- **Scale/Reduce or Enlarge:** This option enables you to increase or decrease the size of your document when it prints. Increasing the size of a document to fill a sheet of paper, especially when it contains a graphic, can decrease the quality.

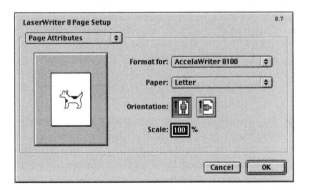

3. Click OK to save your settings.

Printing

You can print most pages, files, and windows on your iMac. If you see a Print command in the File menu (or see a Print button), you should be able to print whatever you see on your screen. Keep in mind that you do need to have your printer installed and set up, and the file or document you want to print needs to be set up first, too. (You can find out about those steps in the previous section.)

Choosing print options

Before you can print, your iMac needs to know more information about how you want your page or document printed. To choose printer options, follow these steps:

1. Choose File➪Print.

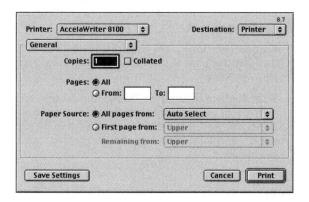

2. In the resulting window, choose your options. Typical options include the following:

- **Number of copies:** You can choose how many copies of a document to print.

- **Page range:** For those documents with more than one page, you can choose to print the pages you want to print. For example, to print just the first page, you would type **1** in the From: box and **1** in the To: box. Some printing options provide a line to enter a range, such as **1-3**, or a noncontiguous range, such as **1, 3, 5**. You may also have the option to only print all odd or even pages, or even all left or right pages (when documents are set up like a book).

- **Quality/Speed:** Select Draft or Econofast for the lowest quality (fastest speed), Normal for average quality (average speed), or Best for best quality (slowest speed). This option is usually available only for inkjet printers.

- **Paper type:** Select the paper type currently in your printer for the best possible image. Paper type is important in inkjet printers because different kinds of paper absorb the ink in different ways.

- **Collate/Back to Front:** This option allows your printed copies to stack in the tray in the proper order.

- **Intensity:** This option enables you to set the darkness of ink or toner.

- **Color matching and halftoning:** You can select the proper setting for photographs or illustrations with shading.

3. Click Save Settings (if available) to make your settings the default.

4. Continue to Step 3 of "Previewing a page" or Step 2 of "Printing a page" in this section.

Previewing a page

On most printers, you can preview your page before it prints. To preview a page, follow these steps:

1. Choose File⇨Print.

2. Set your print options (*see also* "Choosing print options" earlier in this section).

3. Click the Preview button. If you don't have this button, choose File⇨Print Preview. Note that AppleWorks has neither of these options.

After you choose Preview, your iMac displays your page on-screen for you. The on-screen image attempts to show you what your printer can print. Keep in mind, however, that a black-and-white printer can't print in color, even though a preview may show color.

4. Navigate through your document to inspect it. Click the left and right arrows to step through the document (if you have more than one page). You may also type in the number of a particular page. Use the Zoom buttons (the mountain-like buttons) to zoom in and out.

5. Confirm that your document looks the way you want it to look when it prints. If you are not satisfied, click Cancel, make the appropriate changes, and begin again at Step 1.

6. If the preview is acceptable, click the Print button to print one copy of the page you're currently viewing in the preview. Alternately, click Cancel, and skip to "Printing a page."

If your application or printer doesn't support Print Preview, you can use a small utility called Print2PICT by Baudouin Raoult. This application enables you to print a page to an image file or to your clipboard, giving you a preview of the page. You can download Print2PICT at http://thaigate.rd.nacsis.ac.jp/ftp/ upload/krit/thaigfx/Graphics/Print2Pict.html.

Printing a page

Printing a page can be as simple as pressing ⌘+P if you've got your printer and document already set up. If not, see the previous sections in this part for explanations on how to prepare to print. When you're ready to print, follow these steps:

1. Choose File⇨Print or press ⌘+P. Alternately, click the Print button on the toolbar, if available.

2. Click Print or press Return.

3. Watch the screen as your iMac prepares the document's data for your printer and begins sending it. A progress window usually appears to keep you informed of the data submission process.

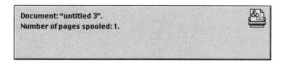

Document: "untitled 3".
Number of pages spooled: 1.

4. If you want to cancel a print job while the data is being sent to the printer, click the Cancel button (if available) or press ⌘+. (period).

If your document is particularly long or contains many graphics, your iMac may take some time to send its data to your printer. If a problem arises in sending your document to the printer, you are informed on-screen and may be given directions on what to do (for example, load more paper if your printer is out).

After your printer receives enough of the data to begin printing, you hear it whir and chug as it applies the image to the paper. Keep an eye on your printed pages as they come out of your printer, too. Paper can jam in the tray and a watchful eye can rescue your print job.

Printing in the background

Your iMac comes with a feature known as *background printing,*
which lets you execute the Print command and then do other
things while your document is processed and printed. Background
printing is usually enabled by default on the iMac, though your
printer may have changed that option. To verify that you have
background printing turned on, follow these steps:

1. Choose the Apple menu⇨Chooser.

2. Select your printer icon on the left.

3. Locate the Background Printing radio buttons on the right. If
the option is off, turn it on by single-clicking the radio button.
If you can't find the Background Printing option for your
printer in the Chooser, check the Print Options window (**see
also** "Choosing print options") and look for a Background
Printing button or menu, or a small icon of a document with a
clock on it.

4. Close the Chooser and confirm your settings if prompted.

With background printing turned on, your iMac sends the data to a
file on your hard drive and then sends that file to your printer in
the background. This means you can do virtually anything else
while your iMac prints. You can even print another document — it
enters a queue and prints after the current document is done. The
only things you can't do while printing in the background is shut
down, restart, or put your iMac to sleep.

Not all printers support background printing, while other printers
require different setup steps to activate it. Check your printer's
documentation for details.

Printing from the desktop

Another way to print documents is to use your printer's desktop
icon. Before you can use this technique, you must first have an icon
on your desktop for your printer. If you don't see one, follow these
steps:

1. Choose the Apple menu⇨Chooser.

2. Select your printer icon in the box on the left.

3. Click Setup and then click Auto Setup.

4. Close the Chooser. Your printer's icon should now be on your
desktop. If it isn't visible, consult your printer's documentation.

To print with your desktop printer icon, follow these steps:

1. Locate the file you want to print on your hard drive.

2. Click-and-drag the file on top of your printer icon — release your mouse button when the printer icon darkens.

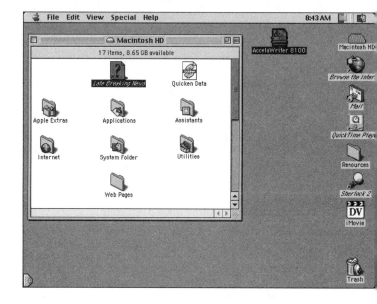

3. Select your print options in the resulting window.

4. Click Print or press Return.

You can use the desktop printer icon to schedule print jobs. Here's how it works:

1. Send a document to the printer through the desktop printer icon or through the Print command in an application.

2. Double-click the desktop printer icon to open the monitoring window and see the list of current print jobs.

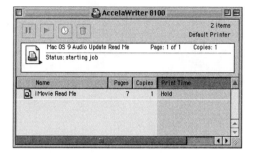

3. Select the job and click the Clock button. The Pause button
    temporarily stops a particular document from printing, the
    Arrow button starts a document printing again, and the Trash
    button cancels a print job.

4. To reorder the print jobs in the queue, click-and-drag a job up
    or down the list and then release the mouse button. Or use the
    Clock button to set a print job to Urgent and move it to the top
    of the list.

5. To stop printing, choose Printing⇨Stop Printing. Choose
    Printing⇨Start Printing when you're ready to resume.

Working with Images

True to its colorful hue and creative shape, you can draw, paint, goof off, and display photos with your iMac. You don't need any special skills or painting smocks, either. Your iMac even comes with the applications you need to get started working with images!

AppleWorks offers drawing and painting spaces, Kid Pix lets you (and your kids) have some imaginative fun with wacky painting tools, and QuickTime offers the ability to view photographs and other images on your iMac.

In this part . . .

Drawing Pictures

You can draw pictures on your iMac using AppleWorks. Drawings are best for things like maps, floor plans, and any images that include text. Drawings use *objects,* which you can manipulate to suit your purpose. Here's how to draw a picture:

1. Open AppleWorks.

2. When prompted, open a new drawing document. Alternately, click the Drawing icon in the toolbar (the icon with a triangle, circle, and square on it).

3. From your drawing tool palette along the left side of your screen, single-click a tool button to select it. This action changes your pointer to the tool in question. You can now click-and-drag the tool across the canvas (screen) to use it.

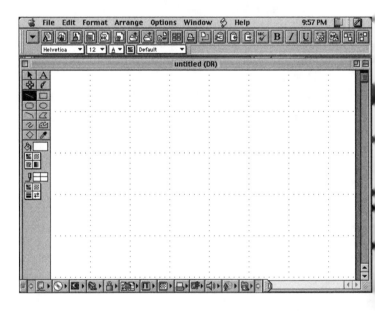

 Most drawing tools are self-explanatory. If you aren't sure what a tool does, choose Help⇨Show Balloons and move your pointer over one of the tools on your palette (but don't click it). A Help Balloon pops up to explain what the tool does. When you're done with the balloons, you can hide them again by choosing File⇨Hide Balloons.

When you create a drawing object with a tool, four black squares appear around it. These black squares are the object's *handles.* Click-and-drag a handle to change the shape of your object.

Handles are always available to resize something on the canvas. If you don't see them, click once on the object to show them again.

To add color, pattern, or texture to a drawing object, follow these steps:

1. Use your arrow tool to select the object you want to modify (single-click it).

2. Single-click one of the two quadrants at the bottom of the drawing tool palette and single-click a color, pattern, texture, or gradient from the resulting palette. The top quadrant fills the object with a color, pattern, texture, or gradient. The bottom quadrant changes the border color, pattern, and width. (The bottom-right button in the lower quadrant applies arrows to straight lines.)

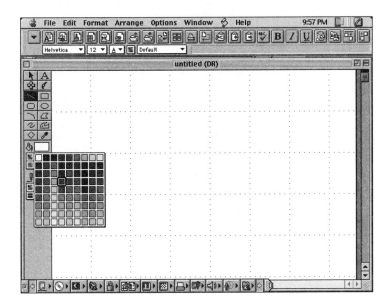

 If you make a mistake, choose Edit⇨Undo or press ⌘+Z to back up one step. Alternately, single-click the incorrect object and press Delete on your keyboard.

Opening Images in QuickTime

To open a graphic image (such as a photograph) in QuickTime, simply try double-clicking the image. If it can be opened on your iMac, the QuickTime Picture Viewer automatically opens or your iMac offers a list of applications that can open it.

To manipulate an image in the QuickTime Picture Viewer, use the options under the Image menu to increase or decrease the size of the image, rotate the image, or flip the image. Regrettably, you cannot save any changes you make to the image in Picture Viewer. If you do need to make and save changes to images, try the GraphicConverter shareware application. You can download GraphicConverter at www.lemkesoft.de.

Painting Images

Painting is best for free-form images, such as sketches and most forms of artistic expression. Painting works with pixels, which are the tiny dots on your screen that make up images. You don't have to paint pixel-by-pixel, but you can if you want. Painting is more challenging but also affords more control. To paint a picture in AppleWorks, follow these steps:

1. Open AppleWorks.

2. When prompted, open a new painting document. Alternately, click the Painting icon in the toolbar (the icon of a paintbrush)

3. From your painting tool palette along the left side of your screen, single-click a tool button to select it. This action changes your pointer to the tool in question. You can now click-and-drag the tool across the canvas (screen) to use it.

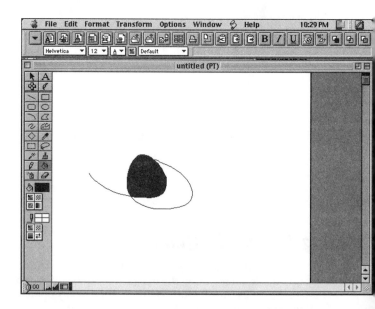

The painting tool palette offers several more tools than the drawing tool palette (which is also in AppleWorks). Here are some of the special painting tools:

- ✔ **Brush:** Select this tool to "paint" on your canvas. To change the width of your brush, double-click the paintbrush tool, select a new brush size (and/or shape), and click OK.

- ✔ **Pencil:** Select this tool to "sketch" on your canvas. Double-click this tool to zoom in on your painting.

- ✔ **Paint Bucket:** Select this tool to fill a bordered area on your canvas. If you use this tool in an area without a solid border around it, your entire canvas is filled with the color, texture, or gradient.

- ✔ **Spray Can:** Select this tool to "scatter" paint in your canvas. To change the spray area and intensity of the spray can tool, double-click the tool, edit the settings, and click OK.

- ✔ **Eraser:** Select this tool to remove parts of your painting. Double-click the eraser tool to erase your entire painting.

Experiment with other tools, colors, patterns, textures, gradients, and so on. Unlike drawings, you must choose your colors, patterns, and so on before you paint. Choosing a color or pattern afterward only affects the next thing you paint.

 If you make a mistake, choose Edit⇨Undo to back up one step. Alternately, click the Eraser tool and click-and-drag it over the mistake in your painting.

Playing with Kid Pix

Most iMacs come bundled with a wonderful painting application called Kid Pix. While the name implies it's just for kids, adults usually find it just as fun as children. Kid Pix does not come preinstalled on your iMac; you must install it yourself. Here's how:

1. Locate and load the Kid Pix CD-ROM disc.

2. Double-click the Kid Pix Studio Deluxe Installer icon when it appears on your screen.

3. Click Continue.

4. Read the text and click Continue again.

5. Click Install. Your iMac displays a progress bar to keep you up-to-date on the installation.

6. When the installation finishes, click OK. You don't need to restart your iMac.

After you install Kid Pix on your iMac, follow these steps to use it:

1. Open the application (double-click the Kid Pix Studio Deluxe icon).

2. If you're asked if you want to switch your monitor to 256 colors, click Switch (or press Return). Kid Pix automatically resets your monitor back to its original number of colors when you quit the application.

3. Click the Kid Pix button from the Picker after the application loads.

The buttons along the left are your main painting tools. Those buttons along the bottom are the options for each tool — different options become available as you select different tools. Use the up and down arrows to cycle through the options.

Kid Pix is an application best explored without too much guidance. It offers surprises and treats around every corner. My recommendation? Try every tool! They must be experienced to be believed!

If you or your kids want to save your creations, choose File⇨Save. You can also export your paintings to GIF or JPEG format by choosing File⇨Export a Graphic.

You can do some amazingly clever things with Kid Pix. Here are some ideas:

✔ **Create a dot-to-dot puzzle:** Select the brush tool, select the "1-2" option at the bottom of the screen (you may have to scroll to find it), and draw a picture. When you release the mouse button, the lines disappear and all you're left with is the numbered dots.

✔ **Color a picture:** Choose Goodies⇨Pick a Color, select a library, and select a picture to color.

✔ **Learn how to pronounce a word:** Choose Speech⇨How to Pronounce, type a word to pronounce, and click Hear Original.

Speech must be enabled for Kid Pix to pronounce a word. Speech is enabled by default. If you disabled the Speech Manager extension, re-enable it in your Extensions Manager.

✔ **Create slide shows with music:** Choose File⇨Return to Picker, click Slideshow, add pictures and music, and click the right arrow to play.

✔ **Have a puppet show:** Choose File⇨Return to Picker, click Digital Puppets, and press keys on the keyboard to make the puppet move.

Understanding Graphic Files

AppleWorks and QuickTime are both capable of opening several types of graphic file formats. AppleWorks can also save documents in some of those formats. If you want to open a graphic file, you usually don't need to understand its format — simply try to open it on your iMac (double-click it). If the file can be opened, either the appropriate application opens automatically or you see a list of applications with which you can open it.

Saving a file in a particular format is a little trickier, however, because you need to understand which formats are best for which purposes. Here is a list of the graphic formats and when you may want to use them:

✔ **AppleWorks:** This is AppleWorks' proprietary graphic format. Use this format when you want to preserve all information in an AppleWorks file. *Note:* You should not use this format when you want to share your file with another person unless you are sure they also have AppleWorks.

✔ **BMP:** This is the Windows native graphic format. Use this if you plan to give a graphic to someone using Windows. *Note:* This format is uncompressed and can be very large.

✔ **GIF:** This is a popular graphic format on the Internet and is compatible with many applications and computers. Quality is not high, however; it's best suited for line drawings. Use this if you want to exchange files across the Internet.

✔ **JPEG:** This is a very common format and often the best all-purpose format. JPEG is a compressed format, however, and isn't ideal if you're overly concerned with quality. JPEG is an excellent choice if you plan to transfer photographs across the Internet or post them on a Web page.

✔ **PICT:** Your iMac's native graphic format. PICT isn't used by many other computer systems. PICT is uncompressed, so the files can be quite large.

✔ **TIF:** A high-quality, compressed image format. Use the TIF format if you plan to have your images reproduced on a printing press.

Making and Watching Videos

A re you ready for the latest wave in computer multimedia? Your iMac is!

With an iMac DV and a DV-capable camcorder, you can import, edit, and create movies. You can even add titles, transitions, music, and sound to your movies using iMovie, a full-featured, movie-editing application that comes with iMac DV models. When you're done, you can export your movie and share it with family and friends.

Every iMac with an Internet connection can watch live news broadcasts, music videos, and movie trailers thanks to QuickTime TV. You just connect to the Internet, select a channel, and watch and listen!

In this part . . .

Connecting Your Camcorder to the iMac DV

If you have a DV-capable camcorder or VCR, you can connect it to your iMac DV. At the time of writing, over 25 camcorder models are DV-capable, including models from Sony, Canon, Panasonic, and Sharp. Not sure if your camcorder is supported? Look for the FireWire symbol (shown below) on your camcorder's video input/output port.

FireWire

Don't see the FireWire symbol? On some camcorders, this port is called iLink or IEEE 1394 port. Still not sure? Open the iMovie Read Me file in your iMovie folder for a list of supported camcorders.

If your camcorder isn't DV-capable, all is not lost. You can purchase a special converter to import your movies into your iMac. You can purchase a special converter box for 8 mm, Hi8, VHS, or SVHS formats. At the time of writing, only the Sony DVMC-DA1 offered this capability, but other models may become available soon.

When you're ready to connect your camcorder, follow these steps:

1. Turn off both your camcorder and iMac.

2. Locate the FireWire cable that came in your iMac DV's Accessory Kit.

   The two ends of the cable are different — one end has a connector with six pins, while the other end has a connector with four pins.

3. Plug the six-pin end of the cable into one of your two FireWire ports on your iMac DV. These ports are located in your access panel on the lower right side of your iMac. Do not force the connector into the port, because it is fragile. Use the alignment notch on the connector and port to help you determine which way to insert the cable.

4. Plug the four-pin end of the cable into the respective port on your DV camcorder or DV device.

5. Turn on your iMac and camcorder/device.

Set your camcorder or power adapter's power switch to VTR mode. If you use the Charge mode during the connection process, your camcorder may not turn back on.

Disconnecting Your Camcorder

Do not disconnect the camcorder from your iMac while importing or exporting movies in iMovie. This could damage your movie files. When you're ready to disconnect, follow these steps:

1. Save all open movie files and quit the iMovie application.

2. Click-and-drag your camcorder's icon on the desktop to the Trash.

3. Choose Special⇨Shut Down to power down your iMac.

4. Unplug the connector from the FireWire port on your camcorder and your iMac. Store the FireWire cable in a safe place for the next time you need it.

Editing Videos with iMovie

One of the most powerful features of iMovie is its ability to edit video clips. Here's how to start:

1. Open a project with movie clips, or create a new project and import clips.

2. Click the blue Edit Mode button below the video viewing monitor (the button has a small image of three movie film frames on it).

3. Click a movie clip on the right to begin editing it.

In the following figure, the large video viewing area in the upper-left corner of the screen is called the *monitor.* The blue line below the monitor is the *scrubber bar.* The area with the small clip images on the right is called the *shelf.* And the gray bar at the bottom of the screen is the *clip viewer.*

Arranging clips into a movie

If you import two or more movie clips, you can arrange these clips to create a single movie. Here's how it works:

1. Click-and-drag a clip from your shelf to the clip viewer.

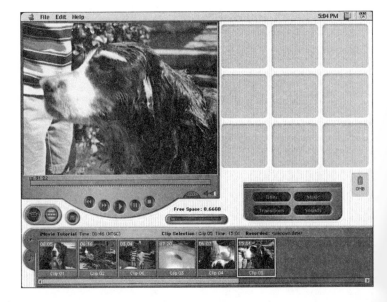

2. Repeat as necessary until all clips you want to arrange into your movie are in the clip viewer. Note that you can click-and-drag clips before or between clips already in the clip viewer.

3. Rearrange any clips by clicking-and-dragging forward or backward in the clip viewer.

4. To view your movie from start to finish, click the blue Play Movie button below the video viewing monitor (the button has an image of a small monitor or TV on it). Your movie plays back on your screen — press any key to interrupt it and return to editing.

Cropping video clips

To crop (remove extraneous data), follow these steps:

1. With a movie displayed in the monitor, locate the segment of the clip you want to keep using the playback controls or by single-clicking on the long, blue bar under the image (the scrubber).

2. Single-click just below the scrubber at the start of the segment you want to keep. Two small triangles appear below the scrubber, indicating the start of the crop.

3. Click-and-drag the right (end) triangle to the end of the segment you want to keep. The portion between the two triangles turns dark blue to indicate that it is selected.

4. Fine-tune the start (left) and end (right) triangles until the segment between them is exactly the part you want to retain.

5. Choose Edit⇨Crop to remove any portion of the video clip that is not selected.

If you want to keep a copy of the unedited video clip for other uses, make a copy of the clip before you crop it. To duplicate a clip, select it on the right or at the bottom, choose Edit⇨Copy, and then choose Edit⇨Paste.

Enhancing movies with music

You can easily add music to your movies. Here's how:

1. Insert an audio CD into your CD-ROM drive.

2. Click the Music button.

3. Select the track on the CD that you'd like to add from the list.

4. Click-and-drag the track to the music track at the bottom of
your clip viewer. Alternately, you can click the Play button in
the music palette until you hear the segment you want to
record, click the Record Music button, and then click the Stop
button when you want to stop recording.

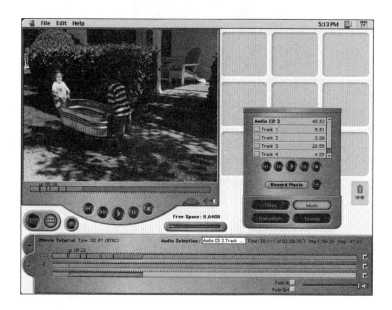

The music clip appears in your music track in your clip viewer after
it is imported or recorded. You can move and edit it as necessary.

To decrease the length of the music clip after it is in your clip viewer,
click-and-drag the triangles at either end to the desired length.

Enhancing movies with sound effects

To add a sound effect to your movie, follow these steps:

1. Click the Sound button.

2. Select a sound effect from the list to hear it.

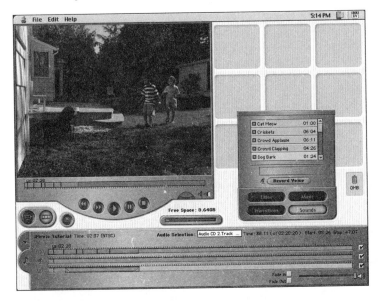

3. Click-and-drag the sound effect you want to use from the list to the sound/narration track in your clip viewer. Alternately, you can click Record Voice to record your own sound effect using your built-in Mac microphone.

The sound effect or voice file appears in the sound/narration track of the clip viewer. You can move and edit it as you like.

Splitting one clip into two clips

To divide one clip into two separate clips, follow these steps:

1. Select the clip on the shelf on the right or in the clip viewer at the bottom.

2. Locate the point in the clip where you want to split it and single-click at that point on the scrubber bar.

3. Choose Edit⇨Split Clip at Playhead.

A new clip appears, containing the second half of the clip. The first half is in the original video clip.

Titling a movie

To add a title to your movie, follow these steps:

1. Select the video clip you want a title to appear in.

2. Single-click the scrubber bar below the video viewing monitor to indicate the exact point you'd like the title to appear.

3. Click the Titles button on the right side of the screen. A palette of options appears.

4. Type the title you want to appear in the boxes near the bottom of the palette.

5. Select the title effect you want in your movie. You can choose from a simple effect like Centered Title to a fun effect like Flying Words. A preview of the title you select is displayed to help you choose.

6. Select a font for your title from the drop-down menu.

7. If you want to move your title to a different position, you may be able to nudge left, right, up, or down with the blue arrows. Not all titles can be moved, however.

8. Single-click the Over Black option if you want your title to appear over a black background.

9. Single-click the Color option and select a color if you want to change the color of your title.

10. Choose a duration for your title display by clicking-and-dragging the duration slider bar (below the Preview/Update buttons). As you drag the slider, the exact duration appears in the lower-right corner of the preview window.

11. Click the Preview button to get a sneak peek at your title.

12. When you're satisfied with your title choices, click-and-drag the title from the effect list to the front of the desired clip in the clip viewer.

Your title appears as a clip in the clip viewer. If you need to modify your title, select it in the clip viewer, click the Titles button, and make your changes.

You can use the title feature for more than just a title at the start of your movie. You could add a location title to a scene that may not be immediately recognizable (such as "Mohave Desert, 1999"). If your movie contains foreign languages, use a title to add a subtitle or two for the benefit of those who do not understand the language.

Transitioning between clips

To add a transition between two clips in a movie, follow these steps:

1. Click the Transitions button.

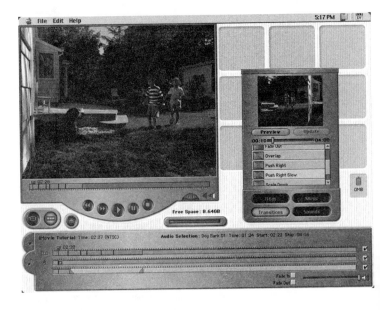

2. Choose a duration for your transition by clicking-and-dragging the duration slider below the preview area. Note that your duration must be shorter than the clip it transitions from in order to work.

3. Select a transition effect from the list to preview it.

4. After you are satisfied with your transition, click-and-drag it from the list to a point between two clips in your clip viewer.

Exporting Movies

After you create your movie in iMovie, you can export it into QuickTime format so that you can share it with others who can view QuickTime movies. Here's how to do it:

1. Open your movie project in iMovie.

2. Choose File⇨Export Movie.

3. Choose Export To⇨QuickTime.

4. Select a format from the Formats drop-down menu. If none of the formats meet your needs, you can choose Expert and select your own image and audio settings.

5. Click Export to begin converting the movie to QuickTime format. This can take a considerable amount of time, depending upon the length of your movie and the export format you chose.

After you export your movie, simply double-click its icon to watch it with the QuickTime Player.

Movie titles may not be legible at low-quality export formats, such as E-mail and Web.

Importing Videos into iMovie

After you connect your camcorder to your iMac, follow these steps to capture a DV clip:

1. Open iMovie.

2. Select New Project in the window that appears. If the window doesn't appear, or iMovie is already open, choose File⇨ New Project.

3. Type a name for your new project and save it.

4. Click the blue Camera Mode button below the main video viewing monitor. The button has a small image of a camcorder on it.

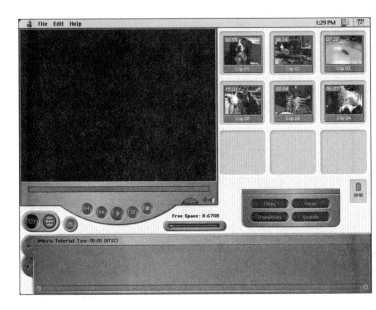

5. Use the playback controls below the main viewing area to move to the desired location in the movie on your camcorder. If you connected your camcorder to the iMac through a DV-capable device, you need to use the controls on your camcorder to navigate through your movie.

6. Rewind your movie to a few seconds before the point where you want to begin importing and click the Play button.

7. When your movie displays the scene you want to import, click the Import button. Alternately, you can press the space bar to being importing.

8. When the movie or scene is finished, click Import again to stop importing. Alternately, you can press the space bar again.

Your imported movie clip appears on the *shelf* (the area with gray boxes on the right side of the screen) and is ready for you to edit. If no more room is available on the shelf, you can move clips to the picture viewer (the gray strip at the bottom of the screen).

If you have definite scenes in the movie on your camcorder, you can use iMovie's scene detection feature to automatically start a new clip at the scene break. For these purposes, a *scene* is defined as a point where the movie is switched from standby mode to record mode on the camcorder. Here's how to use this feature:

1. Choose Edit⇨Preferences.

2. Click the Import tab.

3. Check the box labeled Automatically Start New Clip at Scene Break.

Movie clips take many megabytes of space on your hard drive. For example, a one-minute-long movie imported from your camcorder could take up to 200MB of disk space! Keep an eye on how much room your movies are taking so you don't fill up your hard drive. If you need more room, you can delete the iMovie Tutorial folder to gain some additional space.

Playing Around with QuickTime

QuickTime lets you view digital video and streaming media on your iMac. This means that you can play QuickTime movies, watch QuickTime TV, listen to special radio broadcasts, and see QuickTime components in Web sites.

Using QuickTime

Your iMac comes preinstalled with two important QuickTime applications: PictureViewer (for viewing images) and QuickTime Player (for viewing movies, listening to radio broadcasts, and navigating through QuickTime virtual reality scenes). For the most part, you don't need to worry about which application to use for which file. The appropriate application automatically opens when you double-click a QuickTime file. To learn more about the PictureViewer, *see also* Part VII.

The QuickTime Player offers the following buttons and options in its player window:

✔ **Play (large arrow facing right):** Single-click to watch a video or hear a broadcast.

✔ **Pause (two vertical lines):** Single-click to stop the playback in place.

✔ **Information (*i* button):** Single-click to get more information about the file.

✓ **Options (four squares):** Single-click for a drop-down palette of additional settings and options, including audio balance, bass, and treble.

✓ **Favorites:** Click-and-drag the three horizontal lines at the bottom of the player window to view your favorite movies and channels (from the Favorites menu).

✓ **Volume (a rotary dial in the bottom-left corner of the window):** Click-and-drag it to increase or decrease the volume.

Other features are available in the QuickTime Player menus. To increase the size of the viewing area, choose Movie⇨Double Size. To add a favorite item to the QuickTime Player so that you can frequent it easier, press ⌘+D.

If you use the QuickTime Player to view streaming media, you may be informed that an upgrade is available at a server near you. If you'd like the free upgrade, go ahead and click Update to get it. You shouldn't confuse this with the upgrade to QuickTime Pro, which carries an additional fee ($30 at the time of writing) but also offers more features. To upgrade to QuickTime Pro, visit www.apple.com/quicktime/upgrade/.

Watching TV with QuickTime TV

QuickTime TV offers a variety of viewing channels. While some live programs are available, this isn't really like TV — you can't see your favorite TV shows or movies with it. You can watch live news and radio broadcasts, music videos, and movie trailers; you can even watch live *Webcasts* of concerts.

To watch QuickTime TV, follow these steps:

1. Connect to the Internet as usual.

2. Point your Web browser to www.apple.com/quicktime/.

3. Select a channel to view.

Your QuickTime Player automatically opens and begins downloading the streaming media data from the Internet. The download may take some time — your player indicates the progress of the download with the bar below the viewing area. Play should begin as soon as the information downloads — if it does not, click the Play button. Radio broadcasts do not show an image; only a status bar.

The quality of the images and sound may be poor, even at your highest possible connection speed. Don't be surprised if words cut out in some broadcasts. The best quality comes from radio broadcasts, which don't need to transmit as much data.

To see more QuickTime TV channels, go to `www.apple.com/quicktime/qtv`.

Managing Your iMac

Your iMac has many small utilities that you can use to personal-ize and customize your computer. These utilities are called *Control Panels* and are easily accessible from your Apple menu. They control everything from your Internet settings to the sound volume and the look and feel of your iMac. They can be fun and easy or detailed and sophisticated.

Use this Control Panel primer when you need to tweak a little here and fine-tune a little there. This part offers information on every Control Panel that comes with the latest iMacs, organized in alpha-betical order.

In this part . . .

Accessing Control Panels

Your iMac stores its Control Panels in the System Folder⇨Control
Panels folder. The easiest and fastest way to access them is to
choose the Apple menu⇨Control Panels and display the Control
Panels submenu. Now, just select the Control Panel you'd like to
open from the submenu.

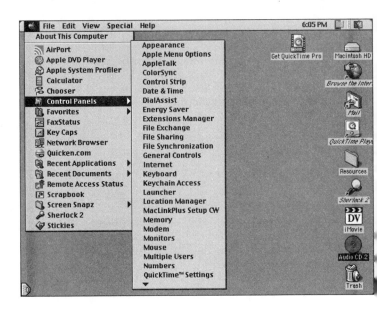

Appearance

You can control and customize the look and feel of your iMac with
the Appearance Control Panel. It offers six categories of controls in
the form of tabs across the top of its window: Themes, Appearance,
Fonts, Desktop, Sound, and Options.

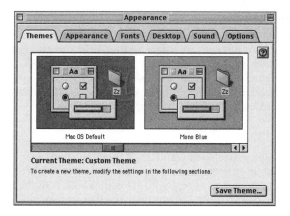

Theme tab

Themes are collections of desktop backgrounds (the image or pattern visible behind the icons), highlight colors (visible when selecting an icon), fonts (shown in the menu bar and menus), and so on. To try on a theme for size, just click it. To create a custom theme, follow these steps:

1. Set each option individually in the other areas of the Appearance Control Panel.

2. Click the Theme tab again.

3. Click the Save Theme button and give your new theme an appropriate name.

Appearance tab

The Appearance tab sets the overall look of menus, icons, windows, controls, and highlight (selection) colors. To create a custom highlight color, select Other at the bottom of the Highlight Color drop-down menu and choose a new color in the resulting window. If you create a dark highlight color, your selected text appears as white.

Fonts tab

The Fonts tab sets the system font (two sizes) and a views font. For optimal readability, or just the classic Mac look, select Chicago. The Smooth All Fonts on Screen option should remain enabled if you want your fonts to look their best.

Desktop tab

The Desktop tab sets the desktop background pattern or image. To set a background pattern, select an item from the list and click the Set Desktop button. To set a background image, click Place Picture, select an image, and click Set Desktop. Be careful not to pick a background image that is too busy — you may not be able to see your icons on it.

Sound tab

The Sound tab accesses your iMac's *sound sets*, which are collections of sound effects that play when you do things like open menus or click buttons. Only one sound set comes with your iMac, but you can download more on the Internet. You may or may not like the sound effects, but enable the sound set for a while to find out.

Options tab

The Options tab offers two important settings. The first, Smart Scrolling, places your scroll arrows at the bottom and right ends of the scroll bars. It also sizes the scroll box relative to the amount of visible information. The second setting lets you collapse windows by double-clicking their title bars. *See also* Part II for step-by-step directions. I recommend that both settings be enabled.

Apple Menu Options

The Apple Menu Options Control Panel changes the way items in your Apple menu appear. It offers two main settings: submenus and recently used items.

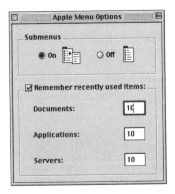

The submenus option is straightforward. If you want submenus to appear in your menus, click the On radio button; otherwise click the Off radio button to disable submenus. If you're unfamiliar with submenus, these are the menus that branch off main menus, allowing you to tunnel down to your target without having to open more windows than necessary. Submenus are enabled by default.

If you want your iMac to keep track of recently used items, keep the Remember Recently Used Items option enabled (checked). You can also specify the number of items remembered from 1 to 99 for the three types of items your iMac tracks: documents, applications, and (network) servers. The default number is 10 for each of the three items.

AppleTalk

Use the AppleTalk Control Panel to select how and where to network your iMac. Your choices from the drop-down menu are Ethernet built-in (for Ethernet networks) and Remote Only (for direct dial connections). You want to select Ethernet Built-In from the drop-down menu if you have one or more of the following:

✔ Your iMac connected to an Ethernet network with one or more other computers.

✔ Your iMac connected to other Macs through AirPort.

✔ Your printer connected to your iMac through an Ethernet hub or Farallon iPrint.

 To learn more about networking, **see also** *The iMac For Dummies,* 2nd Edition, by David Pogue.

ColorSync

ColorSync is a sophisticated technology that ensures color consistency between your screen and your color printer or other color device. ColorSync is of most use to graphic arts professionals using professional-level software (such as Adobe PhotoShop). The majority of iMac users never have need to change these settings; if you do, consult the documentation that came with your color output device or your software. You can also visit www.apple.com/colorsync/.

Control Strip

The primary use of the Control Strip Control Panel is to show or hide your control strip at the bottom of your screen. Just choose the appropriate show or hide radio button.

Control Strip is set to show by default, but you may want to hide it completely or use a *hot key* to show and hide it without having to visit the Control Panel. If you enable the hot key option, you can press ⌘+Control+S to show or hide the Control Strip at any time. To change this hot key combination, follow these steps:

1. Enable the hot key option.

2. Click the Define Hot Key button.

3. Press a new key combination on your keyboard.

4. Click OK.

Each button on the Control Strip offers a quick way to set options you would otherwise have to open a Control Panel to change. To make changes with Control Strip, single-click a button and choose an option from the pop-up menu. Here is a list of the buttons that come with your Control Strip:

 ✔ **AppleTalk:** Toggles AppleTalk on (active) and off (inactive).

 ✔ **CD/DVD-ROM:** Gives you the same options as Apple AudioCD Player, including a track list. You can also turn off and on Autoplay and 3-D Stereo.

 ✔ **Energy Saver:** Opens the Energy Saver Control Panel, toggles between energy conservation and computer performance, and spins down the hard disk or puts your iMac to sleep immediately.

 ✔ **File Sharing:** Shows who is connected to your iMac (at the top of the menu), opens the File Sharing Control Panel, and turns file sharing on and off.

 ✔ **Keychain Access:** Opens the Keychain Access Control Panel, shows keychains, and locks and unlocks keychains.

✔ **Location Manager:** Opens the Location Manager Control Panel and toggles between different locations.

✔ **Monitor Colors:** Opens the Monitors Control Panel and toggles between different monitor color settings.

✔ **Monitor Resolution:** Opens the Monitors Control Panel and toggles between different monitor resolution settings.

✔ **Printer:** Select from available desktop printers.

✔ **Remote Access:** Shows the status of your Internet connection, opens the Remote Access Control Panel, selects between available remote access settings, and connects to and disconnects from your ISP.

✔ **Speakers:** Adjusts the volume up or down.

✔ **Sound In:** Opens the Sound Control Panel and selects from available sound input devices.

✔ **Web Sharing:** Opens the Web Sharing Control Panel and turns Web sharing on and off.

If you find your Control Strip useful, you can also change its font and size to something easier for you to see. The font and size settings affect the menus that pop up when you click a button on the Control Strip.

Date & Time

Use the Date & Time Control Panel to set and adjust your current date, current time, and the menu bar clock.

Setting the current date

To set the current date, single-click the month, day, or year segment in the date field and use the up and down arrows to adjust it. Alternately, you can just type the new number. Use the Tab key to move from number to number in the time field. Alternately, click outside of the date field to set it. The Date Formats button offers a slew of formatting options for your *long date* (weekday, month, day, year) and your *short date* (month/day/year). You can change the separators, enable leading zeros before dates, and show the century. A sample at the bottom of the Date Formats window shows you how your choices look.

Setting the current time

To set the current time, single-click the hour, minute, second, or AM/PM segment in the time field and use the up and down arrows to adjust it. You can use the Tab key to move from number to number in the time field. Alternately, you can type the new number. Click outside of the time field to set it. The Time Formats button lets you adjust the format of your time display — choose from a 24- or 12-hour clock, symbols to use for AM and PM, separators, and leading zeros.

Setting the time zone and daylight savings time

Click the Set Time Zone button to choose your time zone from the list. Most major cities are represented. You can also enable the Set Daylight-Savings Time Automatically option — if you do so, your iMac changes your clock at the correct date and time of daylight-saving time. A check in the Daylight-Saving Time Is in Effect check box tells you whether or not your clock reflects this.

Using Network Time Server

If you want to set your iMac's clock exactly, enable the Use a Network Time Server option. This option compares your clock to a time server on the Internet and updates your clock if a discrepancy is found. Click Server Options to choose your time server, schedule your updates, or manually check and set the time now. *Note:* You must have Internet access to use this option.

Setting up the menu bar clock

The Menu Bar Clock option determines whether or not the clock in the menu bar is displayed. If you turn it on, you can customize the look and feel of it by clicking the Clock Options button and making changes. Options include displaying the time with seconds, showing the day of the week, using a custom clock color or font, and even chiming on the hour, half-hour, or quarter-hour.

)ialAssist

The DialAssist Control Panel stores phone numbers for use with the Remote Access Control Panel. To use it, just enter the appropriate area code, prefix, long distance access number, or suffix (credit card number). You can edit the dialing choices with one of the buttons at the bottom of the Control Panel.

Energy Saver

The Energy Saver Control Panel enables you to adjust when your iMac goes to sleep (low-power mode) and schedule times when it wakes, sleeps, and/or shuts down on its own. To use it, choose the Apple menu⇨Control Panels⇨Energy Saver and click the Sleep Setup button in the upper-left corner if it isn't already selected. If you want to change how long the iMac waits to go into Sleep mode when it is inactive, click-and-drag the slider control on the duration bar. Slide the control all the way to the right if you don't want your iMac to go into Sleep mode automatically. If you want more control, click the Show Details button for more options.

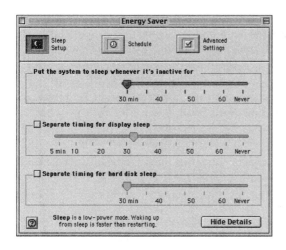

To set your iMac to put the display to sleep before or after the hard disk goes to sleep, or vice versa, enable the appropriate option(s) and adjust the slider control(s).

If you want to schedule automatic wake, sleep, and/or shut down times, click the Schedule button near the top of the window and set the appropriate controls.

The Advanced Settings button offers more sleep and wake options for experts.

Extensions Manager

The Extensions Manager Control Panel allows you to enable and disable system extensions, Control Panels, and startup and shutdown items.

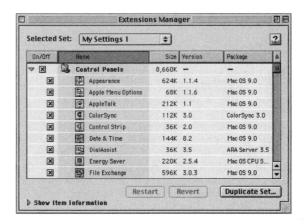

The Selected Set drop-down menu at the top of the Extensions Manager window lets you choose the set of extensions to use or modify. You can't modify locked sets, naturally.

Click the column headings to sort the list by items' status, names, sizes, versions, and packages. The Package field refers to an item's associated software. For example, the ColorSync Control Panel is part of the ColorSync 3.0 package; if you decide you don't need ColorSync, you can disable the entire package.

The Show Item Information toggle at the bottom of the Extensions Manager window displays valuable information about items when selected.

Adding extensions

To add an extension to your operating system, follow the instructions that came with the extension. If none exist, click-and-drag the extension file(s) on top of your System Folder — any extension files are automatically re-routed to the Extensions folder and your iMac informs you of this. After you add an extension to your System Folder, you must restart for the extension to work, in most cases. You do not, however, need to enable the new extension in your Extensions folder — any extension added to the Extensions folder is automatically enabled.

If you want to add an extension but aren't clear on its function, add it to the Extensions (Disabled) folder inside the System Folder. Then choose the Apple menu⇨Control Panels⇨Extensions Manager, highlight the extension, and toggle the "Show Item Information" option at the bottom to learn more about it. If you feel confident enabling it after you understand it better, do so now and click Restart.

Disabling extensions

If you want to disable an item in the Extensions Manager, uncheck the box in the On/Off column to disable it. Turning off extensions and Control Panels in this manner is much better than locating the actual file and dragging it to the Trash. When you disable an item in the Extensions Manager, it is safely moved to the appropriate Extensions (Disabled) or Control Panels (Disabled) folder within your System Folder, where it remains available to enable again if you wish. Changes made in Extensions Manager do not take effect until you restart your iMac.

Finding the extension you seek is often easier if you change your view. Use the Views menu to select a new view. Folder view shows you everything by the folder it is located in (Control Panels, Extensions, and so on). Package view shows you related items (for example, all the America Online-related items). Item view shows everything alphabetically, regardless of folder or package.

Disabling extensions is dangerous, as many applications rely on certain extensions. Exercise this power with caution. If you encounter problems with your settings, you can also select the Mac OS 9 All set from the Selected Set drop-down menu — this option reverts your iMac to its factory settings as far as extensions and Control Panels are concerned.

Managing extensions during startup

To view the Extensions Manager during startup, hold down the spacebar while your iMac powers up. The Extensions Manager dialog box appears, allowing you to enable or disable items before your iMac completes its startup sequence. This is a timesaver, but also a troubleshooting technique when you're having startup problems. After you make your changes, you can click Continue to resume the startup sequence.

File Exchange

The File Exchange Control Panel manages which applications are launched when certain files are opened. It accomplishes two important things: It allows your iMac to read many PC files and it translates most files when the application that created them is missing. Settings for these two functions are under the PC Exchange and File Translation tabs, respectively.

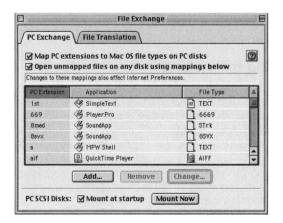

You may add, remove, and reassign PC file types (extensions) to the applications they should open on your iMac. For more information on using File Exchange, click the ? button in the upper-right corner of the dialog box.

File Sharing

File Sharing enables you to change your network identity and password, turn on and off file sharing and program linking, monitor network activity, and define users and groups. The File Sharing Control Panel is only useful if you have a network (Ethernet, AirPort, or TCP/IP).

To learn more about networking, **see also** *The iMac For Dummies,* 2nd Edition.

File Synchronization

The File Synchronization Control Panel synchronizes files and/or folders on the same computer or different computers. The Control Panel itself offers a wealth of information on how to do this (choose Help⇨File Synchronization). Why would anyone want to synchronize files or folders? Good uses of this feature include automatically keeping a current backup of important files and keeping the files on your iMac and iBook the same.

General Controls

The General Controls Control Panel offers six categories of basic settings:

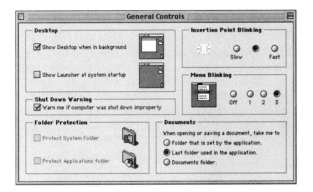

✔ The first desktop option, "Show Desktop When in background," is enabled by default to show the desktop (and its contents) behind any open windows when you're in an application. This means you can switch to the desktop simply by clicking the desktop visible behind the active application. On the other hand, if the desktop distracts you or you find yourself switching to the desktop each time you accidentally click it, disable this option.

✔ The second desktop option shows the Launcher at system startup when enabled. The Launcher is a special window with icons leading to applications all over your hard drive — you can use it to open an application quickly. You can see it by choosing the Apple menu⇨Control Panels⇨Launcher.

✔ Keep the Shut Down Warning option enabled if you want your iMac to warn you on startup if your computer was not shut down properly. At the same time your iMac warns you, it also automatically runs Disk First Aid at startup whenever it detects that it wasn't shut down properly.

✔ Enable the Folder Protection options to safeguard your System Folder and/or Applications folder from accidental deletion. Note that these options are not available if you have File Sharing turned on.

✔ Change the Insertion Point Blinking option to slow down or speed up the rate at which the insertion point blinks. The Menu Blinking option controls the number of blinks you see when you choose a menu item.

✔ The Documents option lets you designate the default folder available from within an application. If you want to save all your documents in the same folder, choose the Documents folder option. Otherwise, the Last Folder Used in the Application option is a good choice.

Internet

The Internet Control Panel stores all your Internet settings and configurations. The easiest way to get any necessary information into the Control Panel is to use the Internet Setup Assistant (Macintosh HD⇨Assistants⇨Internet Setup Assistant). Most of the information you provide in Internet Setup Assistant finds its way into this Control Panel.

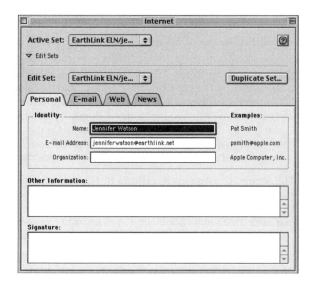

The Internet Control Panel offers four different categories of information: Personal, E-mail, Web, and News. Most items in the Control Panel should already be properly set, but you may want to do the following:

✔ **Create an e-mail signature:** Click the Personal tab and, in the bottom box, type the text that you want to appear at the end of your e-mail messages.

✔ **Change your default e-mail program:** Click the E-mail tab and select a new Default E-mail Application from the drop-down list at the bottom. This updates the Mail alias on your desktop, too.

✔ **Change your default Web browser:** Click the Web tab and select a new Default Web browser from the drop-down list at the bottom. This updates the Browse the Internet alias on your desktop.

Keyboard

The Keyboard Control Panel lets you customize your keyboard with the following options:

✔ **Keyboard Layouts:** This option lets you select a different layout template. Chances are good your iMac is already configured to the layout that works best for you, but if not, this is where you can change it. To see the differences between other layouts, select the layout from the list and choose the Apple menu⇨ Key Caps.

✔ **Key Repeat Rate:** You can change the speed at which a key you're holding down repeats its letter, number, or symbol. Just click-and-drag the slider control left or right. Decrease the rate if you're a slower typist, or increase it if you're a speed typist.

✔ **Delay Until Repeat:** This option lets you adjust the amount of time before a key begins to repeat — click-and-drag the control to Off if you don't want to repeat a character accidentally.

✔ **Function Keys:** Map your function keys (the half-size F keys at the top of your keyboard) to actions. To map a key, click a function key button, select the file, application, or server you would like the function key to open when you press it, and click Assign. Alternately, you can click-and-drag an item into the function key's field to set it.

✔ **Options:** Click this button in the lower-right corner to set the keyboard shortcut to rotate to the next keyboard layout (if you selected more than one). Note that a Keyboard menu appears next to your Application menu when you select more than one keyboard layout, too.

Keychain Access

The Keychain Access Control Panel organizes your encrypted file and server passwords in a safe place. The keychain itself requires a password for access, naturally. If you have passwords to store, and you store them in a keychain, the result is that you really only need to remember one password — that of your keychain. Several areas that require or offer password protection also allow you to add the password to your keychain, such as a password-protected server. Look for a small check box labeled "Add to Keychain" in password windows.

The first time you open Keychain Access, you're prompted to create a keychain. If you do so, be sure to choose a password you can remember. If you forget your keychain password, you're out of luck.

Subsequent visits to the Keychain Access Control Panel allow you to unlock, view, and lock your keychain. To unlock it, click the Unlock button and type in your password — if you get the password wrong, you can try again, but the iMac makes you wait increasingly longer each time you get it wrong. After you unlock a keychain, you see a list of stored password-protected items — to actually view a password, double-click an item, click View Password, and type your keychain access password. When you're done viewing your keychain, you should lock it to keep others from seeing what items you've protected. To lock your keychain, just click the Lock button.

To find out how to encrypt files and add their passphrases to your keychain, *see also* Part III. To learn more about Keychain Access in general, open the Control Panel and click the ? button.

Launcher

This Control Panel simply opens the Launcher window, which is a simple navigational aid. *See also* Part I for more info on the Launcher.

Location Manager

The Location Manager Control Panel organizes your preferences for various settings and controls and saves them, allowing you to restore them quickly or switch between different ones. The

Location Manager is really intended for iBook and PowerBook users, because it enables them to change their settings and controls as they change their location. Nonetheless, iMac folks may find uses for it as well. To create a new Location, open the Control Panel and choose File⇨New Location. You can learn more about Location Manager by clicking the ? button.

Memory

Your Memory Control Panel controls the amount of memory allocated to disk cache, virtual memory, and RAM disk.

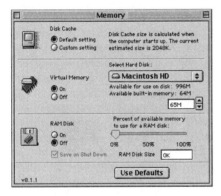

Changing disk cache

The *disk cache* is temporary memory set aside for actions that need speed. Disk cache contents are erased when you restart, shut down, or crash. Most likely, the default setting is also the best setting. If you are instructed to modify your disk cache or just want to try out a new setting, follow these steps:

1. Open the Memory Control Panel.

2. Click the Custom Setting radio button.

3. In the resulting warning window, click Custom again.

4. Adjust the cache size with the up and down arrows.

 A large disk cache holds on to information longer than usual. This is a problem if you crash, because data you added or modified recently may not have been saved to your hard drive yet.

 If you have a RAM disk (detailed later in this part), the percentage of total available RAM needed for it increases as you increase your disk cache. That's because your disk cache uses RAM, too.

Changing virtual memory

Your iMac comes with virtual memory already turned on. You can turn it off, though I don't recommend it unless you're specifically instructed to do so. Your iMac and its applications seem to work best when virtual memory is on. You may want to increase the hard drive space dedicated to virtual memory, however, but only if you feel you need it. Here's how to do it:

1. Open your Memory Control Panel.

2. Verify that your virtual memory is enabled (if it isn't, turn it on).

3. Click the up or down arrows to increase (or decrease) the total amount of virtual memory you want available. A single megabyte of virtual memory is the bare minimum, though. For example, if you have 64MB of RAM, you can have 65MB or more of combined RAM and virtual memory. You can go higher than double your built-in memory — any more than that and your iMac may slow to a crawl.

4. When you complete your virtual memory setup, restart your iMac — your virtual memory won't be available until you do.

When your iMac finishes restarting, check About This Computer under the Apple menu. The Virtual Memory field indicates the total amount of memory you now have. You may want to increase some of your application's memory allocations now to take advantage of your "new" memory (see "Setting application memory" later in this part).

Checking built-in memory

To check the amount of built-in memory in your iMac, open the Memory Control Panel and note the number after "Available built-in memory." That's your built-in memory size. You can also get this figure by choosing the Apple menu⇨About This Computer.

If you want to add more built-in memory to your iMac, you can! To learn how, visit www.apple.com/support/ and click the iMac Support hyperlink and then the Adding RAM hyperlink.

Setting application memory

To change an application's memory allocation, follow these steps:

1. Quit the application of which you want to adjust memory allocation.

2. Select the application's icon.

3. Choose File⇨Get Info⇨Memory. Alternately, press ⌘+I and choose Memory from the drop-down list.

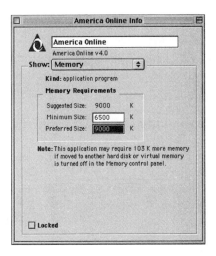

4. In the resulting dialog box, locate the Preferred Size field and double-click it to select its contents.

5. Type a new number. If you're not sure what to change it to, consider increasing the preferred size amount by 25 to 50 percent over the suggested size. You probably won't want to go over that amount, unless specifically instructed to do so. Any memory you allocate to an application is devoted exclusively to it while it is running and isn't available to any other application(s) that may need it.

6. After you set your preferred size, change your minimum size to the same amount.

7. Close the Get Info window. Your changes take effect the next time you launch the application.

Using RAM disks

RAM disks are portions of your built-in memory (RAM) set aside to use like a hard drive. They are very fast, and best used when you want to speed up an application you're using intensively. RAM disks are an advanced feature — please use caution when creating and using them. To create a RAM disk, follow these steps:

1. Open your Memory Control Panel.

2. Click the On radio button under RAM disk.

3. Click-and-drag the slider control to indicate how much of your RAM you want to use as a RAM disk. I do not recommend that you use all your available memory for a RAM disk; doing so has been known to cause problems.

As you slide the control, the Disk Cache size and Available Built-In Memory amounts change accordingly.

4. Make sure the "Save on Shut Down" option is enabled to preserve your RAM disk (and contents) when you shut down your iMac.

5. Restart your iMac.

Upon restart, your RAM disk appears on your desktop as an icon that looks like a floppy disk with a RAM chip on it.

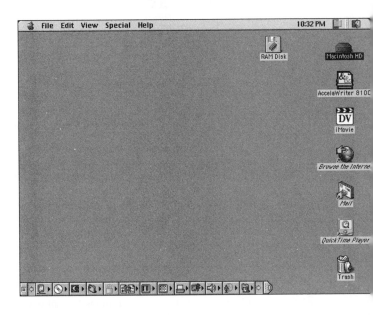

Double-click the RAM disk icon to open it as you would your hard drive and copy items onto it. Try copying an application you use frequently to it. You may use the application you copy to your RAM disk immediately, and any data saved to the RAM disk is secure unless you trash it or turn off the RAM disk. Using applications on RAM disks works just the same as on your hard drive — double-click the application's icon to open it. You don't need to copy documents over to the RAM disk, and I wouldn't recommend it in the event you turn off the RAM disk before you back up the document.

When you restart or shut down, your iMac saves a copy of everything on the RAM disk. This process takes a few moments — your iMac changes your pointer to a miniature version of the RAM Disk icon as a visual clue that it is saving this information. When the process is complete, your iMac restarts or shuts down as you requested. When your iMac powers up again, your RAM disk is intact along with all its contents.

To remove a RAM disk, revisit your Memory Control Panel, click the Off radio button under RAM Disk, and restart your iMac.

When you remove a RAM disk, all the contents of the disk are lost.

Modem

Use the Modem Control Panel to set your sound and dialing options. If you use America Online to access the Internet, you may never need to use this Control Panel. EarthLink and other ISP users may find uses for the options, however. Here's what you can do in the Modem Control Panel:

✔ To select a new modem (when you install a new modem, for example), choose it from the drop-down modem list.

✔ To turn off your modem's screeching sounds, click the Off radio button.

✔ To change your dialing from tone to pulse, and vice versa, click the Tone or Pulse radio buttons. (Tone and pulse are dialing methods used by your phone company. Most phones these days use tone; if you have pulse, you'll know it.)

✔ To have your modem dial without regard to the dial tone, check Ignore dial tone. This is useful when you're using a business telephone system with deceptive dial tones, for example.

Monitors

The Monitors Control Panel lets you customize the appearance and performance of your monitor (display). Three buttons across the top offer Monitor, Geometry, and Color settings.

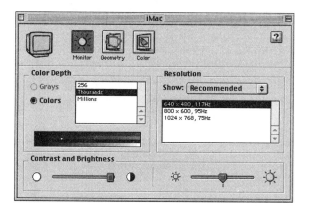

✔ **Monitor:** You can change the color depth (the number of color
displayed). Select Thousands or Millions for the best effect.
Select 256 for faster performance and memory conservation.
Resolution options let you change the number of pixels displayed on your screen — the lower the number, the bigger
everything will be (and the less room you have to work in). A
good compromise between available real estate with readabilit
is 800 x 600. Contrast and Brightness controls let you adjust th
monitor for optimal viewing.

✔ **Geometry:** These controls let you adjust the display's position
on the monitor. Click the buttons beside and below the representation of the monitor to increase or decrease the height an
width of your screen. The usual goal is to fill as much of the
screen as possible, without losing quality, of course.

✔ **Color:** This control lets you select your ColorSync profile,
which is used in desktop publishing and graphic packages for
matching on-screen color to color output. The Calibrate butto
at the bottom guides you through the color adjustment
process, if you're so inclined.

Mouse

The Mouse Control Panel adjusts tracking and click speed. Just
click-and-drag the slider controls as needed. If you're new to the
iMac, you may get best results with a slower tracking speed and
slower double-click speed (move the slider controls to the right).

Multiple Users

A new feature of Mac OS 9, the Multiple Users Control Panel lets
you set up your iMac so that other people in your home or office
can use it — all without having to worry about sensitive information or personal settings. To set up Multiple Users, follow these
steps:

1. Choose the Apple menu⇨Control Panels⇨Multiple Users.

2. Turn on Multiple User Accounts by clicking the On radio
button at the bottom of the window.

3. Click the New User button.

4. Click Show Setup Details at the bottom of the window.

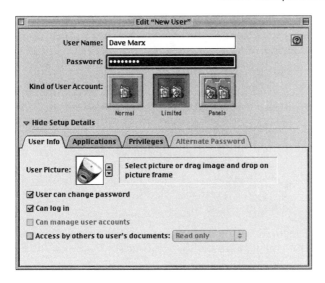

5. Type the name of the person who will be using your iMac.

6. Type a password they can remember (nothing too easy, of course).

7. Select the kind of user account that is appropriate to the person. A Normal account has no restrictions on applications and may have restrictions on other user's documents. A Limited account lets you disallow access to applications you choose and lets you set privileges for certain things, like playing CD-ROMs. A Panels account is the simplest — the person sees only two panels on the screen: One panel lists their allowed applications and the other panel lists their documents.

8. Click the User Info tab and select the appropriate options.

9. If you choose a Limited or Panels account, click the Applications tab and select the applications that this person is allowed to use. Alternately, you can click Select All or Select None.

10. If you choose a Limited or Panels account, click the Privileges tab and select the privileges.

11. When finished, close the Edit New User window to save your settings.

12. Restart your iMac.

When your iMac powers up again, it displays a list of users. You can select yourself (you're the owner) or your new user, type the password, and log on.

You can set more options for yourself and your users, including alternate passwords. Here's how:

1. Revisit the Multiple Users Control Panel.

2. Click Options on the right.

3. If you so desire, type a welcome message for your users, set log-in settings (including the ability for users to speak their user name and password), or create a list of CD/DVD-ROMs that certain users may be restricted to. You can set a bunch o. other options as well.

To learn more about speaking your username and password (voice print verification), *see also* The iMac For Dummies, 2nd Edition.

Multiple Users is a very full-featured Control Panel — click the ? button to get more information on how to make the most of it.

To see your options as an owner in Multiple Users, double-click your name (or "owner") in the list. Note that you should set a pass word for yourself.

Numbers

The Numbers Control Panel lets you set your number format pref-erences. Most likely the Control Panel is already set exactly where you want it by default, but feel free to change the format, separa-tors, and currency if you need something different.

QuickTime Settings

The QuickTime Settings Control Panel lets you configure QuickTime. For the most part, the defaults should be configured correctly. If you want to change how CDs behave when you first load them into your iMac, select AutoPlay from the drop-down menu at the top of the window.

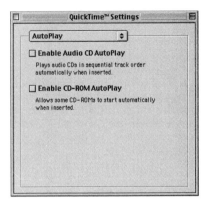

 You can choose to disable AutoPlay of audio CDs and/or CD-ROMs (they are enabled by default). Consider disabling these options so that the infamous Autostart virus cannot infect your iMac.

Remote Access

Remote Access provides control of your ISP Internet connection, as well as the ability to connect to another Mac remotely. Most iMac users only need to use it to connect to their ISP. If you do have an ISP account, click the Setup toggle — your username and access number should be listed here, as well as your password if you have it saved. Use the Connect button at the bottom to dial up and connect to your ISP. Once connected, a Disconnect button becomes available — click it if you're ready to get offline.

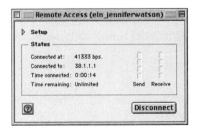

The Options button lets you set redial, connection, and protocol settings. To learn more about Remote Access, click the ? button.

 If you only use Remote Access to connect and disconnect from your ISP, choose the Apple menu⇨Remote Access Status instead. It offers a small window and those same handy Connect/Disconnect buttons.

Software Update

A new Mac OS 9 feature, Software Update checks for newer versions of your system software. You need an Internet connection to use this Control Panel. Just open the Control Panel and click the Update Now button. It connects you to the Internet (assuming your Internet settings are correct), compares your software versions with the current versions, and lets you know what it found. You have the choice to actually download and install the new software. Click an update to learn more about it.

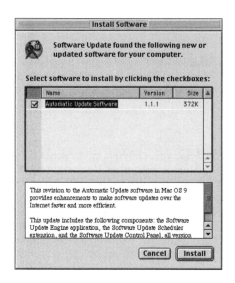

You can also choose to schedule automatic software updates — just enable the option and click the Set Schedule button to set it up.

Sound

The Sound Control Panel offers volume adjustments, alert sound selections, and speaker setup.

To change your sound volume, open the Sound Control Panel, click Output from the list on the left, and click-and-drag the slider control along the bar. If you want to turn your sound off completely, click the Mute check box.

To adjust the volume and/or balance of your speakers, click Speaker Setup from the list on the left of the Sound Control Panel, and click-and-drag the left and/or right speaker slider control along the bar. Use the Start Test button at the bottom-right of the window to test the volume and balance of the two speakers.

To record a new alert sound, follow these steps:

1. Select Alert Sounds on the left

2. Click Add.

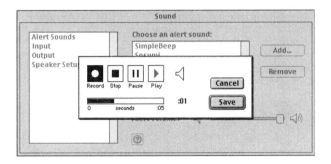

3. Click Record when you're ready.

4. Speak, play, or otherwise make your sound.

5. Click Stop when finished.

6. Click Play to hear your sound.

7. If you're satisfied with your new sound, click Save to name your sound. If you're not satisfied, repeat Steps 3 through 6.

Note that new alert sounds are automatically selected in the alert sound list.

Speech

The Speech Control Panel lets you choose your iMac's speaking voice and configure talking alerts. Use the drop-down menu at the top to toggle between Voice options and Talking Alert options.

Voice options control the sound of the voice and the rate at which it is played. Use the Voice drop-down menu to select a voice from 25 possible voices, which range from serious (Bruce and Victoria, for example) to silly (Bad News and Deranged). The rate slide control changes the speed at which the voice is heard. If you find it hard to understand the voice, try slowing it down.

Talking Alert options change if and how your iMac speaks alerts that appear on your screen. (Alerts are things like "Are you sure you want to quit?") If you aren't always watching your screen, talking alerts can be quite useful, but mostly they are fun, or at worst, annoying. Play around a bit with it to see if you like it.

In both the Voices and Talking Alerts options, the small speaker icon lets you listen to the changes you make.

Startup Disk

The Startup Disk Control Panel lets you select the hard drive or disc to start from the next time you power up.

If you have only one hard drive, chances are you'll just want to keep that selected. If you have an external hard drive with a System Folder on it, select that icon in this Control Panel and the next time you start your iMac it starts up with the operating system on the external hard drive. You can also start from CD-ROM discs if the disc has a System Folder on it (as your iMac Install disc does).

TCP/IP

The TCP/IP Control Panel stores settings for connecting to the Internet via an Internet service provider. If you're using AOL instead, you should have AOL Link Enhanced selected in the Connect via drop-down menu. Click the ? button to learn more about your TCP/IP settings.

Text

The Text Control Panel lets you choose between languages installed on your iMac. Most people never need to use this.

Web Sharing

Web Sharing lets you make a folder on your hard drive available to anyone who dials in to your iMac. To learn more about it, search the Help Center for "Web Sharing."

Troubleshooting

Sooner or later, something goes wrong. Even iMacs are subject to Murphy's Law. What's more significant is that you have ways to troubleshoot your problems and plenty of resources to call upon.

If you experience freezes, crashes, startup problems, printing problems, lost or orphaned files, or just need to find help, this is the place to be. In this part, you find step-by-step directions to get you up and running again quickly. Don't neglect to look for additional assistance in obvious places, such as in the documentation that came with your iMac and in other software, too!

In this part . . .

Finding Lost Files

If you can't find a file, Sherlock 2 probably can. Here's how to search for a file with Sherlock 2:

1. Choose the Apple menu⇨Sherlock 2. Alternately, if you're on the desktop, press ⌘+F.

2. Type the filename you think you may have used. For example, if you are missing a letter you wrote to your friend Ann, type **Ann**.

3. Select the File Names radio button, if it isn't already enabled.

4. Click the magnifying glass icon (find).

Sherlock 2 displays your results in the bottom half of the window. If that produces too many results (you may find files with names like Annual Report or Banner), try searching for your file based on the date it was last modified. Here's how:

1. Click the Edit button on the far right of the Sherlock 2 window.

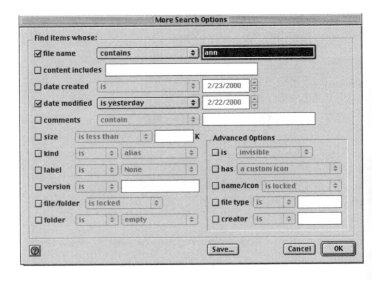

2. Click the "date modified" check box.

3. Select an appropriate time frame from the drop-down menu to the right of "date modified." For example, if you worked on your file yesterday, you would want to select "is yesterday" from the menu.

4. Click OK to save your settings.

5. Click the magnifying glass again to re-search for your file.

This time, the results include all files modified yesterday. Your file is bound to be in that list somewhere, probably with a name you wouldn't expect.

 If Sherlock 2 doesn't turn up your missing file, open the application with which you created your missing file and choose the File menu. Some applications list recent documents at the bottom of the File menu and you may find your missing file. Another idea is to choose the Apple menu⇨Recent Documents to see if your file is listed there.

Finding More Help

If you've tried everything but still can't successfully troubleshoot your iMac's problem, try these additional help resources:

✓ **Press ⌘+?.** This keyboard shortcut opens a help file. Also look for ? buttons in various windows — these usually lead to task-specific help. Your iMac offers extensive help databases under the Help menu on the desktop.

✓ **Visit Apple's Web site.** Apple offers software updates, an extensive technical information library, peer-to-peer assistance, and plenty of articles and tips for making the most of your iMac. Their Web site is located at www.apple.com.

✓ **Visit other support Web sites.** If your problem is specific to a particular application, visit its Web site — virtually every application and utility has some form of technical support (or at least information) on the Web. Check the documentation that came with your iMac for support information, or search for the product name on the Web with Sherlock 2.

✔ **Visit guru Web sites.** You can get some of the best *guru* help around at the hundreds of Mac sites created and maintained by fans. To find a list of them, search for "iMac" at www.yahoo.com. For specific help with troubleshooting, visit www.macfixit.com

✔ **Use Apple Technical Support.** Your purchase of an iMac entitles you to 90 days of free technical support from Apple. It begins on the date of your computer purchase. Phone numbers and additional Apple support options are available on the Apple Service and Support Guide that came with your iMac. Use this as a last resort, when the above solutions don't help and/or you're unable to turn on your iMac. If you use up your 90 days of free support, consider the AppleCare Protection Plan — for about $150, you get three more years of support and repairs. The catch? You must purchase AppleCare prior to the expiration of your one-year limited warranty.

Fixing Printing Problems

If your iMac tells you that your printer "could not be opened" (or found), try these solutions:

✔ Check that your printer is turned on and properly connected to your iMac.

✔ Choose the Apple menu⇨Chooser and select your printer icon again (for more details on how to do this, *see also* Part VI).

✔ If your printer is connected to your iMac via a network, be sure AppleTalk is turned on and your network is functioning. You may need to turn your network hub and/or bridge off and on again.

If you send a file to the printer but nothing happens, try these solutions:

✔ Double-click the printer icon on your desktop, choose the Printing menu, and verify that a check mark appears next to Start Print Queue (if it isn't there, select Start Print Queue to enable it). Alternately, choose Applications Menu⇨ PrintMonitor and confirm that printing is enabled in your PrintMonitor and that data is being sent to your printer.

✔ Be patient. Sometimes a document takes a while to send to your printer and you simply need to give it some more time. Long files or those with complex graphics can take five or more minutes.

If nothing else works, zap your PRAM. What in the world does that mean? I explain in "Speeding Up Your iMac" later in this part.

Opening Orphaned Files

If you double-click a file and a dialog box tells you that "the application could not be found," follow these steps:

1. Select the file icon in question.

2. Press ⌘+I.

3. In the resulting Get Info dialog box, check the Kind field. This may tell you what kind of application created the file.

4. If you have this application listed in the Get Info dialog box, locate and open the application and then try to open the document within it.

If you don't have the application that created the file, you can try to open it from within a similar application. As a last resort, try rebuilding your desktop — I detail how to do that in "Speeding Up Your iMac" later in this part.

Resolving Extension Conflicts

An *extension conflict* occurs when one or more of your system extensions conflict with one another or with other applications on your iMac. Extension conflicts usually happen on startup, when your iMac announces that a "system error has occurred" and stops functioning. If you think you have an extension conflict, follow these steps:

1. If your computer is "frozen" (no movement on-screen), restart your computer using the techniques described in "Resolving Startup Problems" later in this part.

2. As your iMac restarts, press and hold down the Shift key until you see the message "Extensions Off." This allows your iMac to start without extensions.

If your problem was an extension conflict, your iMac should be able to finish its startup sequence without problems. Unfortunately, all your extensions are disabled, which means no faxes, no e-mail, no CD-ROM discs, and so on. To pinpoint the exact extension conflict and resolve it, follow these steps:

1. Choose the Apple menu⇨Control Panels⇨Extensions Manager.

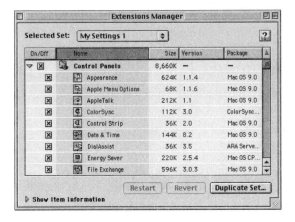

2. In the resulting dialog box, turn off half of your extensions by clicking on the check boxes.

3. Click Restart at the bottom of the Extensions Manager window. Allow your iMac to start normally (do not hold down the Shift key this time).

If everything goes smoothly, you know that your problem resides with at least one of the extensions you turned off (if it doesn't, turn off some more extensions and restart again).

4. Return to your Extensions Manager and turn half of those you turned off back on again, and restart again.

5. Repeat until you hone in on the problem extension. Keep in mind that your problem may be between two extensions, but at least you'll find one of the problem extensions this way and can then repeat the procedure to find the second one.

6. When you find the conflicting extensions, turn off the extension you don't need.

7. Close Extensions Manager and restart once more.

Resolving Startup Problems

If your iMac doesn't do anything when you press the power button, try these solutions:

✔ Check that your iMac is actually plugged into a wall outlet — if you use a surge protector, verify that it is turned on and plugged in, too.

✔ If you pressed the power button on the keyboard, verify that the keyboard is plugged into the iMac — if it is, try the power button on the iMac instead.

If you see a flashing question mark icon when you press the power button, try restarting your iMac. Here are the possible ways to force a restart:

✔ Press the power button on your iMac again.

✔ Press and hold the Control and Option keys while pressing the power button.

✔ Press the restart button near the bottom of your access panel (the button with the triangle on it).

✔ If you don't see a restart button in your access panel, look for a very small hole (the one with the small arrow above it) between your phone jack and your Ethernet jack. This is the restart hole on some iMacs. Straighten out a paper clip and insert it into this hole, pushing firmly (but not forcing it) until your iMac restarts.

✔ Press and hold the power button on your iMac for five seconds.

✔ As a last resort, unplug the iMac power cord.

If a restart doesn't solve your problems, try starting up from a CD-ROM disc. Here's how:

1. Locate your iMac Install CD-ROM disc and insert it into your iMac.

2. Restart your iMac (use the previous techniques if necessary).

3. Press and hold the C key while your iMac powers up. The C key tells your iMac to use the software on the CD-ROM disc rather than the software on your hard drive.

4. If your iMac successfully starts up, open your Utilities folder and run the Disk First Aid application. If problems are detected, try to fix them and restart your iMac.

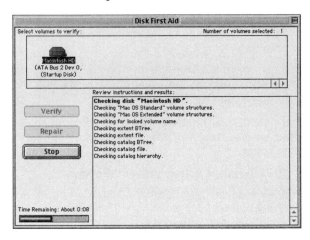

5. If your iMac cannot start up, try to reinstall the operating system from the iMac Install CD-ROM disc. For further assistance, contact Apple Technical Support (*see also* "Finding More Help" earlier in this part for more information).

If your iMac doesn't boot up off the CD-ROM, then you have a hardware problem. Your best bet is to call Apple Technical Support immediately.

If you press the power button, the monitor comes to life, but you don't hear the customary chime, try these solutions:

- ✔ Check that your sound is turned on (choose the Apple menu⇨ Control Panels⇨Sound).

- ✔ Remove any headphones you may have plugged into your headphone jacks.

- ✔ Verify that any external speakers you may have installed are turned on and their sound volumes are turned up.

If you press the power button and your iMac informs you that a "system error has occurred" or something along those lines, *see also* "Resolving Extension Conflicts" earlier in this part.

Speeding Up Your iMac

If your iMac slows down suddenly, you may be on the verge of a crash or freeze. To decrease risk to your data and correct the problem, first save any open files and quit all open applications, then immediately restart your iMac. Restarting resolves many speed issues that are related to memory problems.

If you notice a gradual slow down over the weeks and months that you use it, try these solutions:

✔ **Rebuild your desktop file.** The invisible desktop file can become unwieldy over time, causing your iMac to slow down or have icon problems. To rebuild the desktop file, restart your iMac (or power it up if it is off) and hold down the ⌘ and Option keys until asked if you want to rebuild your desktop. Click OK and sit back while your iMac rebuilds it (which can take a while if you have a large hard drive).

✔ **Defragment your hard drive.** You need to purchase a separate utility application to do this, such as TechTool Pro or Norton Utilities. I advise that you defragment your hard drive occasionally.

If you notice problems with settings, printing, or networks, you may need to *zap* your PRAM (or parameter memory — a special form of memory powered by your iMac's battery). Here's how to do it:

1. Restart your iMac.

2. During restart, press and hold the ⌘, Option, P, and R keys.

3. Release the keys when you hear the second chord.

You may need to reset Control Panels, printers, and networked computers afterwards. At the very least, you need to reset your time zone in the Date and Time Control Panel after you zap the PRAM.

Some weekly preventative maintenance on your iMac can go a long way toward avoiding the problems mentioned in this part. Apple suggests rebuilding your desktop and zapping your PRAM on a weekly basis. If you do these regularly, consider using TechTool, which will do it for you faster and easier. You can download a free-ware version (re: simplified version) of the utility at www.micromat.com. If you elect to get AppleCare, a special version of TechTool Pro comes with it; this version has many more features than the freeware version, though not as many as the full-blown version. If you go with AppleCare and get your limited edition of TechTool Pro, you can easily upgrade to the full version for about $50 (at the time of writing).

Surviving Freezes and Crashes

A *freeze* is when everything on your iMac comes to a standstill. Your pointer may or may not move, but it can't select anything. A *crash,* on the other hand, is when your iMac announces that something has gone wrong. It may inform you that an application has unexpectedly quit or simply that a system error occurred. If you encounter a freeze or crash, try these solutions:

🖝 Verify that your keyboard and mouse connections are secure. If not, secure them.

🖝 Press ⌘+. (period) at the same time.

🖝 Press Option+⌘+Esc all at the same time. A dialog box should pop up, asking you if you want to "force" the application to quit.

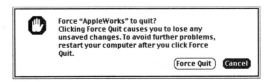

Force "AppleWorks" to quit?
Clicking Force Quit causes you to lose any unsaved changes. To avoid further problems, restart your computer after you click Force Quit.

(Force Quit) (Cancel)

You could click Cancel, but it probably won't matter at this point. Go ahead and click Force Quit. About half the time the application actually quits and dumps you back to the Finder. If this happens, save any work open in other applications, quit those applications, and restart your iMac immediately.

When you force-quit an application, you lose whatever work you've done since the last time you saved the document. Yet another reason for the mantra "Save early and save often."

🖝 As a last resort, restart your computer (*see also* "Resolving Startup Conflicts" earlier in this part).

Part XI

Mac OS 9 Command Reference

C urious about your desktop menus? Want to learn more about a command before you initiate it? Wondering about the new features in Mac OS 9?

You can learn the ins and outs of each menu item on the Mac OS 9 desktop here! This part lists each menu and menu item in alphabetical order to help you look up your command quickly.

In this part . . .

Apple Menu⇨About This Computer

About This Computer displays basic information about your iMac. Information includes the OS version, built-in RAM size, and virtual memory size, among others. One of its most useful features is a list of the currently running software and the amount of RAM being used. If you're running several applications at once and become concerned about running out of available memory, check About This Computer.

Apple Menu⇨Apple System Profiler

Apple System Profiler displays detailed information about your iMac. Think of it as About This Computer on steroids. It looks closely at your system, devices and volumes, control panels, extensions, applications, and System Folder(s) and reports back numbers, versions, manufacturers, and so on. The uses for this utility are endless, and you may be called upon to use this if you contact Apple Technical Support. If you've been itching to peek under the hood of your iMac, spend some time wandering around Apple System Profiler.

If you see a small triangle beside a word, single-click it to see more information.

Apple Menu⇨Calculator

What computer isn't complete without a calculator? Your iMac has a tidy, little one that does simple calculations. Click the digit buttons in the calculator window to enter numbers, or simply press the keys on your keyboard. For example, to add three numbers, do this: Press the first number, press the + key, press the second number, press the + key, press the third number, and press the = key. Voila! To clear the calculation, press C or the Clear button on your keyboard.

If you want to copy a number displayed in the calculator window, just press ⌘+C. You can paste it back into your calculator later or into a document in another application.

Apple Menu⇨Chooser

The Chooser lets you select a printer or network to use. To use it, open the Chooser, click an icon in the left box, and click a resulting option on the right. Refer to Printing Documents for more details on selecting and configuring printers in the Chooser.

If your iMac is networked with one or more computers, follow these steps to connect to one of them:

1. Open the Chooser.

2. Click the AppleShare icon.

3. Select a file server in the list on the right.

4. Indicate your status (guest or registered user) and type your name and password (if known) into the text entry boxes. Contact your network administrator if you're unsure of your status, username, or password.

5. Click Connect to initiate a connection.

6. In the resulting window, select the hard drive(s) you wish to use. To select more than one at once, hold down the Shift key.

7. Click OK.

Apple Menu⇨Favorites

The Apple menu is a collection of favorite places on your iMac. Whenever you come across something you'd like to add to this list, choose File⇨Add To Favorites. This menu item isn't always available, however, so you can't add every favorite thing to your Favorites List. When feasible, this is a good alternative to adding something to the Apple menu itself.

Add your hard drive to the Favorites menu. If you have submenus enabled (in your Apple Menu Options Control Panel), you can now use the hard drive link in your Favorites list to navigate down several levels without opening windows.

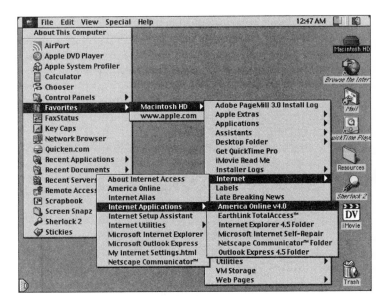

Apple Menu⇨Key Caps

Can't remember how to make the Σ symbol? Check Key Caps. This nifty little utility shows you the character behind each key on your keyboard.

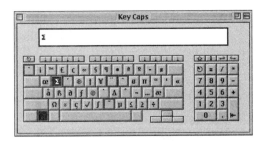

To use it, just press a character on your keyboard to see it represented on-screen. Press the Shift key to see what character you can make when you press Shift+*character*. Try the Option key, and

Option+Shift, too! You can even use the Font menu to change the font to match the one you're using in your document. If you find the character you're seeking, you can select it in the window, copy it, and paste it into your document.

 Another way to create special characters is to use the Symbol or Zapf Dingbats fonts, which come preinstalled on your iMac. Select these fonts from the Fonts menu in Key Caps to see the wide variety of additional characters.

Apple Menu⇨Network Browser

The Network Browser is useful for connecting to servers on AppleTalk (the Mac computer network protocol) and on the Internet. If your Internet Control Panel is configured for an ISP or other Internet connection, opening the Network Browser either initiates a connection or shows you the networks to which you can connect.

Apple Menu⇨Recent Applications

The Recent Applications submenu near the bottom of your Apple menu lists the applications you last opened. Just select one from the submenu to open it. If you'd prefer to see more or less applications in this list, choose the Apple menu⇨Control Panels⇨Apple Menu Options and edit the number of applications you want your iMac to remember. Use your Recent Applications submenu to return to frequently used applications quickly and easily.

Apple Menu⇨Recent Documents

Your iMac keeps a list of the documents you've opened recently in the Recent Documents submenu. Select a document from the submenu to open it, automatically opening the appropriate application (if it isn't already open). To see more or less documents in this submenu, choose the Apple menu⇨Control Panels⇨Apple Menu Options and edit the number of documents you want your iMac to remember. Use this submenu as a shortcut to your favorite documents.

Apple Menu⇨Recent Servers

Servers you've connected to recently are recorded in the Recent Servers submenu. If you routinely connect to the same servers, this little list can really speed up the process of connecting to servers!

Apple Menu⇨Scrapbook

The Scrapbook can keep a permanent record of your text, images, sounds, and even movies and three-dimensional objects. To store something in the Scrapbook, follow these steps:

1. Select the item you want to save.

2. Choose Edit⇨Copy.

3. Choose the Apple menu⇨Scrapbook.

4. Choose Edit⇨Paste.

To retrieve something from the Scrapbook, do this:

1. Choose the Apple menu⇨Scrapbook.

2. Use the scroll bar along the bottom to locate the item.

3. Choose File⇨Copy. The lower portion of the Scrapbook window lists details about the item selected. Note that sounds can be played and three-dimensional objects can be navigated using the controls built right into the Scrapbook!

4. Paste the item into your document.

Apple Menu⇨Sherlock 2

Sherlock 2 is a powerful searching feature of Mac OS 9, upgraded from Sherlock available in Mac OS 8. You can search filenames, file contents, and Internet content — all from within Sherlock 2. New features in Sherlock 2 are more in-depth custom searches, faster file content searches, and channel (category)-based Internet searches. To learn more about Sherlock, ***see also*** Parts IV and X. Also visit www.apple.com/sherlock/.

Apple Menu⇨Stickies

If you find those little yellow sticky notes helpful, why not use them on your iMac, too? Stickies is a nifty little program that lets you create your own sticky notes and place them right on your iMac desktop. To use Stickies, choose the Apple menu⇨Stickies, choose File⇨New Note (or press ⌘+N), and type your note.

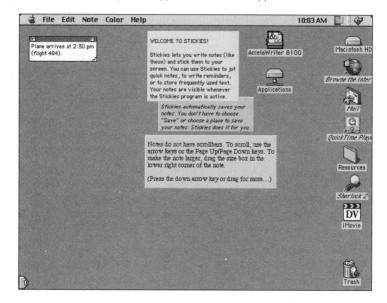

You can reposition your note by clicking-and-dragging the bar at the top around your screen. Stickies are saved automatically for you, too!

If you close a Stickie window using the Close box, you are prompted to save your note as a text file, but not as a Stickie file. Thus, don't close a Stickie window until you are finished with it and have no need to see it as a Stickie note again.

If you find Stickies helpful, consider placing an alias to it in your Startup Items folder inside your System Folder. This opens Stickies each time you restart your iMac, meaning you're more likely to see all those reminders you make for yourself! If you're not sure how to do this, here's a shortcut: Choose Edit⇨Preferences, enable the "Launch at system startup" option, and click OK.

Application Menu⇨"Application List"

The Application menu (at the far right end of your menu bar) displays a list of applications at the bottom of the menu. Any open application on your iMac shows up in this list. Use the list to switch to another application or just to see what applications you have running.

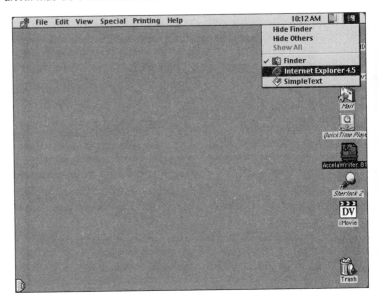

The Application menu's name or icon indicates the application you're currently running. To toggle between showing the application name and icon, click-and-drag the vertical line to the left of the menu name.

To switch to an application while hiding all other applications in the background, hold down the Control and Option keys while you select an application from the menu.

Application Menu⇨Hide Finder/"Application"

Have you ever been caught playing a game at work or working on a surprise for someone who just walked in the room? You could just press ⌘+Q to quit it quickly, but you could lose unsaved work and you'd need to reopen it again later. A better alternative is to *hide* the application. Hiding simply means removing the windows from your screen without actually closing the windows or quitting the application. To hide the application you're currently using, choose the Application menu⇨Hide *Application*. The menu item name includes your active application. For example, if you're playing in Kid Pix, you would see Hide Kid Pix in the Application menu.

Hiding an application makes another application active on your screen.

Application Menu⇨Hide Others

If you have a lot of clutter in the background behind your active application, hide the extraneous windows by choosing the Application menu⇨Hide Others. If you still see the icons on your desktop and would rather not, you can hide these also by choosing the Apple menu⇨Control Panels⇨General Controls and disabling the "Show Desktop when in background" option.

Application Menu⇨Show All

Wondering where all your application windows went? Choose the Application menu⇨Show All to display all open windows in all your open applications.

Edit⇨Clear

The Clear command permanently deletes selected text and some other items. Clear doesn't work on everything — you can't use it to delete a file, for example. Use Clear when you have large blocks of text that you want to remove with one fell swoop.

The Clear command is permanent. If you want to save a copy of the item you're removing, use the Cut command instead.

Edit⇨Copy (⌘+C)

The Copy command records the selected text or item and places it on your Clipboard for later use. The *Clipboard* is an electronic holding area, which is also sometimes called a *buffer*. To view your Clipboard, and thus the text or item you copied, choose Edit⇨Show Clipboard.

The Clipboard can hold only one item at a time. If you copy something, and then copy something else, the first thing you copied drops out. So only the last item you copied is actually on your Clipboard. Also, if you restart your computer, your Clipboard is cleared.

Edit⇨Cut (⌘+X)

The Cut command removes the selected text or item, but stores a copy of it in the Clipboard for later use. Use Cut when you want to delete something, but then paste it back in somewhere else.

Edit⇨Paste (⌘+V)

The Paste command places the contents of the Clipboard at your text insertion point or other selected area. You use the Paste command after copying or cutting something. If the Paste command is unavailable, that means you have nothing on the Clipboard that can be pasted.

Edit⇨Preferences

The Preferences command displays your desktop settings, which are organized into three categories: General, Views, and Labels. **See also** "Setting Desktop Preferences" in Part I for details on each preference.

Edit⇨Select All (⌘+A)

Use the Select All command to select all text in a document or all items in a window. For example, if you open the Macintosh HD and choose Edit⇨Select All, each file and folder in the window becomes highlighted (selected). Even if you don't want every item selected, you can use this command and then hold down the Shift key while single-clicking specific items to unselect them.

Edit⇨Show Clipboard

You can see what you've stored on your Clipboard at any time by choosing Edit⇨Show Clipboard.

The Clipboard window appears and displays its current contents, whether it be text, a graphic, or another item. Check the message below the title bar for the item's type.

If your Clipboard is empty, your Clipboard window is empty and a message to that effect appears below the title bar.

Edit⇨Undo (⌘+Z)

Use the Undo command when you want to back up a step. For example, if you accidentally cut something instead of copy it, choose File⇨Undo to restore the item. The trick is that you can undo only the previous action, though some applications, such as Microsoft Word, let you go back and undo several actions in a row. If Undo cannot be selected, you can't undo whatever you did.

If you undo something and then decide you really did want to do it, don't worry. Just revisit the Edit menu again before doing anything else and select Undo again.

File⇨Close Window (⌘+W)

Use the Close Window command to close an open window on your desktop. If you hold down the Option key while you choose the File menu, the Close Window command changes to Close All and closes every window on your desktop if selected. (Option+⌘+W does the same thing.)

File⇨Duplicate (⌘+D)

The Duplicate command creates copies of files and folders on your desktop. Just select an item and choose File⇨Duplicate — a copy appears beside the original, with the word *copy* appended to the end of the filename. This command won't work on the hard drive icon or the Trash icon, naturally.

File⇨Encrypt

The Encrypt command is a new security feature added to Mac OS 9. Using Encrypt, you can password-protect a file quickly and easily. It only works with document files, however, so this command is only available after first selecting a file on your desktop. To encrypt, select a file, choose File⇨Encrypt, and type a passphrase (password).

When you first use the Encrypt command, you are asked if you want to create a keychain to store passwords. Your iMac uses the keychain to store the passwords you give to encrypted files. When you create the keychain, you are asked to name it and give it a password. If you do create a keychain, don't forget your password — there is no way to retrieve it if you do.

File⇨Find (⌘+F)

The Find command opens Sherlock 2, mentioned earlier in this part. If you frequently use Sherlock, learn the keyboard shortcut (⌘+F) to open it quickly. To learn more about using Sherlock 2, *see also* Part II and Part IV.

File⇨Get Info (⌘+I)

Get Info is actually a submenu within the File menu. As the name implies, it offers information about items on your iMac. The contents of the submenu vary from item to item, though you can get General Information on any item on your iMac. You may also see a Sharing option, which offers information on whether the information is being shared across a network and who can read and write to it. Items that require memory management, such as applications, have a Memory option in the Get Info submenu — it is used to check and change memory allocations.

To use, select an item, and press ⌘+I. When the Get Information window opens, you can access the informational categories with the drop-down menu at the top of the window.

If you use Get Info on an alias file, a new button appears in the bottom-right corner: Select New Original. Click this button to re-link the alias to a new file. For example, if you have an alias called "Homework" that points to a folder with May's school assignments, you could click Select New Original to re-link the alias to a folder with June's school assignments instead.

File⇨Label

Use the Label command to select a label for an item on your desktop. Labels are used to organize and categorize information. You can change label names and colors in Edit⇨Preferences.

File⇨Make Alias (⌘+M)

Use the Make Alias command to create an alias of a file or folder. To use, select a file or folder on the desktop and choose File⇨Make Alias. Your iMac places a new alias file beside the original file — the alias file's label appears in italics with the word *alias* appended to the end. You can now rename and/or move the alias file wherever you wish.

If you want to create an alias of a file in a different folder, hold down the Option and ⌘ keys as you click-and-drag the original file to the destination folder. This automatically creates an alias of the file in the destination folder.

To learn the location of the original file that your alias points to, select the alias, press ⌘+I, and note the location after Original. To actually see the original file, choose File⇨Show Original.

File⇨Move To Trash (⌘+Delete)

Use the Move To Trash command in lieu of clicking-and-dragging a file or folder to the Trash icon. This command is most useful when you use its keyboard shortcut: ⌘+Delete. To use this command, select the file or folder, and press ⌘+Delete. To actually delete an item from your computer, you must also choose Special⇨Empty Trash.

File⇨New Folder (⌘+N)

Use the New Folder command to create a new folder on your desktop. To use it, open the hard drive or folder in which you would like your new folder to appear, choose File⇨New Folder, and then immediately type a new name for your folder.

You can click-and-drag your new folder to another location after creating it, if you wish. You can also create a new folder on the desktop by clicking anywhere on your desktop's background before issuing the New Folder command.

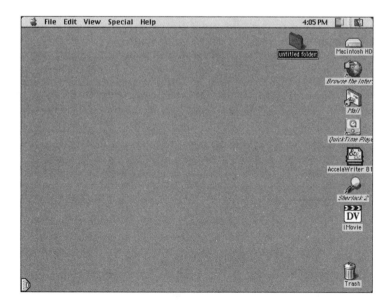

File⇨Open (⌘+O)

Use the Open command in lieu of double-clicking icons to open folders, files, and applications. This command is most convenient when you use its keyboard shortcut: ⌘+O. To open more than one item at a time with this command, select a group of items by holding down the Shift key while you single-click each one, and then press ⌘+O.

File⇨Page Setup

Before you print, use the Page Setup command to choose paper size, orientation, scale, and other options that may be available for your printer. *See also* "Setting Up a Page" in Part VI for more details on Page Setup options.

File⇨Print (⌘+P)

Use the Print command to print documents right from the desktop. Just select a document, choose File⇨Print, and click Print when the application opens and presents the print options window. To print a group of documents from the desktop, hold down the Shift key to select all the documents you want to print, and then choose File⇨Print (or press ⌘+P). *See also* Part VI for more information on printing from the desktop.

File⇨Print Desktop/Window

Would you like to save a copy of your desktop for future reference? Single-click once on your desktop background, choose File⇨Print Desktop, and press Print. If you just want to print one window on your desktop, single-click that window and then choose File⇨Print Window. Your printed image should look nearly identical to what you see on-screen, with the exception of your desktop background.

If the entire desktop won't fit on one piece of paper, you may have the option to scale the window down before you print it. Choose File⇨Page Setup and look for a scale option.

File⇨Put Away (⌘+Y)

If you move a file or folder to the desktop for convenience and later want to return it to its original folder, use the Put Away command. Your iMac tracks the movements of files and folders, so it can always remember where to put away a file or folder. Put Away even works after you shut down or restart your computer!

 The Put Away command also works on removable media, such as CD-ROM and DVD-ROM discs — it works the same as choosing Special⇨Eject or clicking-and-dragging the disc to the Trash.

File⇨Search Internet (⌘+H)

The Search Internet command opens Sherlock 2 to its Internet searching channel. Use the keyboard shortcut for fast access. **See also** Part IV for more information on searching the Internet with Sherlock.

File⇨Show Original

Use the Show Original command to locate an alias's original file. Just select the alias's icon and choose File⇨Show Original. The iMac opens the folder containing the original file and selects the original file itself.

Help⇨Help Center

Whenever you have a question about how something works on your iMac, choose Help⇨Help Center to access the iMac's help database. The Help Center contains all the iMac-specific help resources, so this is often your best choice when seeking assistance. To use the Help Center, follow these steps:

1. Choose Help⇨Help Center.

2. In the resulting window, type a word or phrase that describes your problem or question.

3. Click Search.

The Help Center displays all matching results in the same window, organized by order of relevance.

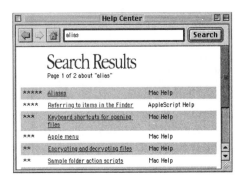

To read a help article, single-click its name (which should be blue and underlined). The article opens in the same window. If you want to go back to the list of results after reading an article, click the arrow facing left. To return to the top of the Help Center, click the Home button.

Help⇨Hide Balloons

Use Hide Balloons to turn off Balloon Help, which is turned on with the Help⇨Show Balloons command. Balloon help provides short descriptions of things on your screen whenever your pointer hovers over them for a moment. Balloon Help can be useful, but very annoying after a while.

Help⇨Mac Help (⌘+?)

Browse and search for Mac-specific help articles with Mac Help. This database is included in the Help Center (Help⇨Help Center), but it is easier to access with the keyboard shortcut: ⌘+?. *See also* "Help⇨Help Center" for details on searching a help database.

Help⇨Mac Tutorials

New to the iMac? Get your feet wet with Mac Tutorials! A set of three tutorials — Desktop Skills, Internet Basics, and Mac Basics — helps you master essential skills, such as moving the mouse/pointer, clicking, working with windows, and editing text.

Help⇨Show Balloons

Use Show Balloons to turn on Balloon Help. With Balloon Help on, you can move your pointer around the screen and get little balloons of information. You need to let your pointer hover over an object for a moment or two before the balloon appears.

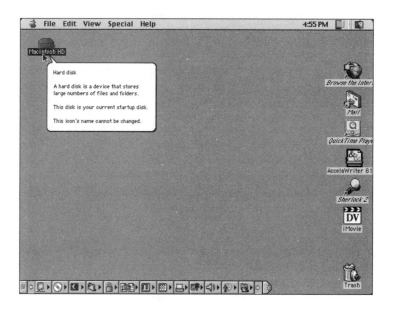

To dismiss the balloon, simply move your pointer away from the object. To turn off Balloon Help, choose Help⇨Hide Balloons.

Special⇨Eject Disk (⌘+E)

To remove or *unmount* removable media (such as CD-ROM discs, DVD-ROM discs, Zip/Jaz cartridges, or floppy disks), you can use the Special⇨Eject Disk command. For CD-ROM and DVD-ROM discs, this command works the same as simply clicking-and-dragging the disc icon to the Trash. If you use this command on a Zip/Jaz cartridge or a floppy disk, however, a ghost image of the icon remains on your desktop even after the cartridge/disk is ejected. This can be a pain or a benefit, depending upon how you use your iMac and your cartridges/disk.

If you use this command to eject a Zip/Jaz disc or a floppy disk, don't double-click the ghost image of the icon trying to open it. Your iMac will prompt you to reinsert the disc, which can be a pain if you can't remember where you put it!

Special⇨Empty Trash

To permanently delete your files queued for deletion in the Trash folder, choose Special⇨Empty Trash. You must empty the trash like this occasionally, or you'll amass a huge number of files that you really just want to delete. Occasionally, your iMac may tell you that a file needs to be trashed immediately and prompts you to do so, but that usually only happens when you're low on disk space. After you select Empty Trash, your iMac asks if you're sure you want to permanently remove the files. If this verification becomes tiresome, you can disable it by selecting the Trash icon, pressing ⌘+I, and disabling the "Warn before emptying" option at the bottom of the window.

 You can retrieve items from the Trash anytime before you issue the Empty Trash command. Just double-click the Trash icon and click-and-drag the desired item to safety on your desktop or to another folder.

Special⇨Erase Disk

Use the Erase Disk command only when you want to completely delete everything on a disk. Do not use this command unless you know exactly what you're doing. The Erase Disk command is most commonly used to reformat floppy disks or Zip/Jaz discs. If you partitioned your hard drive into smaller units with Drive Setup, you may occasionally want to erase a partition. If your hard drive contains no partitions, relax — you cannot erase it accidentally.

Special⇨Restart

When you want to shut down and immediately start up your iMac again, choose Special⇨Restart. This command is most commonly used after installing new software and when you notice slowdowns that may be due to memory issues. Restarting closes all open documents and applications, erases the contents of your Clipboard, and disconnects you from networks and the Internet.

Special⇨Shut Down

When you're ready to shut down your iMac for the day, choose Special⇨Shut Down. This command initiates special shutdown procedures and powers down your iMac. You do not have to unplug your iMac from the surge suppressor or wall outlet after shut down.

Special⇨Sleep

Leaving the iMac but plan to return soon? Choose Special⇨Sleep to put your iMac's hard drive in an energy conservation mode and black the screen. No applications, documents, or windows will be closed during sleep mode. During sleep, the power button on some iMac models flashes on and off slowly to indicate its status. To wake up an iMac that's sleeping, press the power key, press any key on the keyboard, or click your mouse button.

If you leave your iMac unattended or inactive for 30 minutes, your iMac will automatically go into sleep mode. You can change this amount of time by choosing the Apple Menu⇨Control Panels⇨ Energy Saver. **_See also_** Part IX for details on how to configure your sleep options.

View⇨Arrange

The Arrange submenu allows you to organize icons and buttons on your desktop or in a folder by certain criteria, such as name, date modified, date created, size, kind, and label. To use it, single-click the location you want to arrange and choose Views⇨Arrange⇨_Criteria._ Note that if you use this command on the desktop, your hard drive icon(s) always appear at the top far right of the screen regardless of any criteria.

If you want to arrange a group of items in a very specific order that doesn't conform to one of the criteria in the Arrange submenus, apply different labels to the items to force your own organization upon it.

View⇨as Buttons

To see items on the desktop or in windows as buttons, click the area you want to change and choose View⇨as Buttons. Your iMac changes all items in that location to buttons.

What's the advantage? You only need to single-click buttons to open them, unlike icons or list items, which require double-clicks. You may also want to change the size of the buttons with the View Options command, because large buttons take considerable room on the screen.

View⇨as Icons

To see items as icons, choose View⇨as Icons. Use this option when you've changed items in a location to view as buttons or view as a list. Icons are the default on your iMac, unless you create a new folder in a window that is displaying items in another view (in this case, the new folder reflects the settings of its parent folder).

View⇨as List

To see items in a window in List view, choose View⇨as List. List view offers more information in less space and is often preferred by Mac gurus.

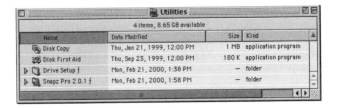

One of the major advantages of List view is the ability to sort infor-mation in the window simply by clicking one of the category headings at the top of the window. You can click the arrow at the far right end of the window to re-sort the information in reverse order, too.

Note that you cannot view items on the Desktop in List view.

'iew➪as Pop-up Window

If you like to keep your desktop organized, consider viewing your windows as *pop-ups*. Just select a window and choose View➪as Pop-up Window. This changes your window's title bar to a tab.

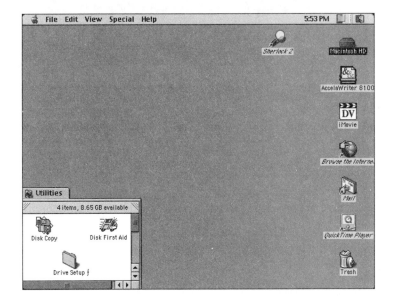

When you're finished using this window, click the tab to collapse the window so that only the tab is visible at the bottom of the window.

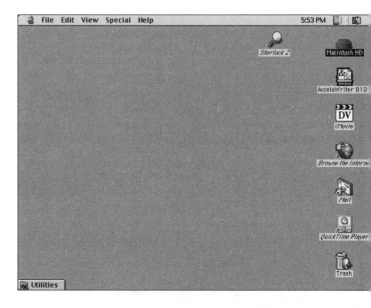

When you want to use the window again, just click the tab again. To change a pop-up window back to a regular window, either make it active and choose View⇨as Window or just click-and-drag it higher on your desktop and release the mouse button.

View⇨as Window

Use this command to change pop-up windows back to regular windows. *See also* View⇨as Pop-up Window to learn more about how pop-up windows work.

View⇨Clean Up

The Clean Up command is a quick way to organize messy icons or buttons in a window or on your desktop. Just select the location you'd like to clean up and choose View⇨Clean Up. Your iMac moves icons into straight lines and columns that would do any housekeeper proud.

View⇨Sort List

The Sort List submenu is available when you have a window displayed in List view. Use the Sort List submenu to pick the criteria by which you'd like items in a list sorted.

You can add and remove criteria in your Sort List submenu by choosing Edit⇨Preferences, clicking the Views tab, and checking or unchecking items under Show Columns on the left side of the screen.

View⇨View Options

The View Options command presents a variety of settings that you can apply to specific windows. To use, follow these steps:

1. Single-click the desktop or window you want to change.

2. Choose View⇨View Options.

3. In the resulting window, make the settings you wish.

4. Click OK to save changes and close the window.

The View Options settings include the following:

✓ **Use relative date:** With this option enabled, dates in the Date Created and Dated Modified columns use the words *today* and *yesterday* instead of today's or yesterday's specific date. In general, this is easier to use, but you may turn it off if you find it bothersome.

✓ **Calculate folder sizes:** Your iMac displays the amount of disk space each folder occupies when this setting is enabled. Calculating folder sizes can slow down your iMac, however, so use this option only when necessary. Note that if you don't have Size enabled under Show Columns on the right, the Calculate Folder Sizes option is unavailable.

✔ **Icon size:** Change the size of your icons to small, medium, or large. This is entirely a personal preference and has little impact on the functionality of your iMac. The default size is medium.

✔ **Show columns:** Enable or disable the information you want to appear in a window displayed in List view. Note that the option selected here determines what criteria you have available in the View⇨Sort List submenu.

✔ **Set to standard views:** Click this button to return the settings to the standard view set in Edit⇨Preferences.

Glossary: Tech Talk

AirPort: A wireless technology that allows AirPort-enabled iMacs to connect to the Internet and other compatible computers. An AirPort Base Station is required and must be purchased separately.

Alias: A file that points to another file, folder, or application located elsewhere on the computer. Selecting an alias has the same effect as selecting the actual item it represents.

Apple menu: The menu on the far left of the iMac menu bar, represented by a multi-colored apple icon. The Apple menu provides access to Control Panels, plus many other important applications and utilities.

AppleWorks: Formerly known as ClarisWorks. An application program combining word processing, spreadsheet, database, communications, drawing, and painting. AppleWorks comes with the iMac.

Application: A computer program (or set of instructions) designed to perform a task or series of tasks unrelated to the fundamental operation of the computer. Common applications include word processing programs, spreadsheets, databases, Web browsers, and games.

Browser: An application program used to view information posted on the World Wide Web. Browsers fetch, assemble, and display Web pages from the many individual files that can make up a single page. The iMac comes with three browsers: Microsoft Internet Explorer, Netscape Communicator, and the America Online browser (which is actually a special version of Microsoft Internet Explorer).

Button: An on-screen representation of a push button that you can activate when you move the pointer over the button and press the mouse button.

Chooser: A utility found in the Apple menu. Used to specify and select the printers (and networks) attached to an iMac.

Click-and-drag: This is the mouse technique used to highlight text and to move selected text or other objects. To click-and-drag, position the mouse pointer over that object, press and hold down the mouse button, move the mouse so that the object is in the desired position, and release the mouse button.

Command (⌘) key: Also known as the Apple key, for the Apple icon it displays. Normally found to the left of the space bar on the iMac keyboard, it's used in combination with other keys to perform a variety of keyboard shortcuts and other functions.

Control key: The Control key is used in combination with other keys to perform a variety of keyboard shortcuts and other functions. Located in the bottom-left corner of the iMac keyboard.

Control Panel: A utility or built-in function used to change settings and features of the computer or specific applications. Control Panel files are found in the System Folder⇨Control Panels, and links to the Control Panels are available by choosing Apple menu⇨Control Panels.

Control Strip: A special collection of small icons found at the bottom of the iMac desktop. The Control Strip supplies shortcuts to certain frequently used features and controls. You can resize it by clicking-and-dragging the tab on the far right end.

Copy: To record data. To copy text, select it and choose Edit⇨Copy.

Cursor keys: A group of four keys that you can use to move the cursor (pointer) around a computer screen, in lieu of a mouse. The cursor keys are up arrow, down arrow, left arrow, and right arrow.

Cut: To record data at the same time you remove it. To cut text, select it and choose Edit⇨Cut.

Data: Information. Data files contain text, images, numbers, sounds, and so on.

Database: An application designed to store and retrieve data in an organized manner, and to analyze and display that data in useful forms. Also, a data file or group of related data files created by a database program, dedicated to a particular purpose. AppleWorks contains a database application.

Delete: To remove information without recording a copy of it. To delete text, select it and press the Delete key.

Desktop: The starting point and central workspace of a Macintosh computer, displayed on the computer's monitor. Like an actual desktop, all your work is done on top of the desktop, and all the facilities, tools, and resources you need are found on the desktop. Also known as the *Finder*.

Dialog box: A small window that appears on-screen to request data input or deliver a message.

Double-click: To press and release the mouse button twice in rapid succession. A double-click on an icon opens a file or runs an application.

Drag: To move the mouse, usually while depressing the mouse button. You can use dragging to select text or to move objects around on-screen.

DVD-ROM: Digital Video Disc-Read Only Memory. DVD discs are used to store video, audio, and data. DVD-ROM drives, such as those in the iMac DV models, can play CD-ROM discs as well as DVD-ROM discs.

mail: Short for electronic mail. Text messages sent between computers and related devices via a network, using a set of standard protocols. Your iMac has three potential e-mail applications: Outlook Express, Netscape Communicator, and America Online.

ncrypt: A new Mac OS 9 feature that encodes data so those who do not know the passphrase are unable to access it. To encrypt a file, select it and then choose File⇨Encrypt.

scape (Esc) key: A key in the upper-left corner of the iMac keyboard. The Escape key is used in conjunction with the Option key and the Command key to force-quit an application that has frozen.

thernet: A communications system that networks computers. Ethernet defines the wiring and electrical characteristics of the network. Ethernet supports the operation of networking protocols, such as AppleTalk and TCP/IP, both of which can operate over Ethernet. The iMac is Ethernet ready.

xtension: An addition to the Mac OS intended to expand its capabilities. Extensions are commonly installed during the installation of a new application program. Extension files are stored in the System Folder⇨ Extensions folder.

Extensions Manager: A Control Panel that helps users identify extensions and resolve conflicts between extensions that may be having a negative effect on the operation of the computer.

File: A collection of data on a computer. Files can contain data or program instructions, and be very simple or very complex. Typically, a single document is stored in a file, but some applications consist of many files.

Folder: A collection of files and/or other folders, used to organize information on the iMac. Mac folders are analogous to folders in a filing cabinet.

Font: An electronic file that defines a particular style of type to display and print text. Also refers directly to the distinctive style of that type.

Force-quit: The process of forcing an application to close, usually when you can't use File⇨Quit. To force-quit, press and hold Option+⌘+ Esc. Use force-quit only as a last measure.

Gigabyte: One billion bytes. A gigabyte is typically used to measure the size of a hard drive, as in "My iMac has an 8 gigabyte (or 8GB) hard drive." Abbreviated as "GB" or "gig."

Graphic: An image, such as a drawing, painting, or photograph.

Hard drive: A device for the storage of computer data. Every iMac comes equipped with a hard drive, which stores the data for the Mac OS, application programs, and data files. Files stored on a hard drive are copied into RAM for use and computation, and the results are recorded on the hard drive. Information on a hard drive remains intact when the power is turned off.

Highlight: To select a block of text on-screen. To highlight text, click-and-drag the pointer across the desired text and release the mouse button. Highlighted text appears as light text against a dark background. Highlighted text may be dragged to another location, copied, deleted, or reformatted.

Home page: The first Web page displayed by a Web browser. Home page may also refer to an individual's personal Web site.

HTML: Hypertext Markup Language. HTML is the system used to create and display Web pages. Adobe PageMill helps users create HTML.

http: Hypertext Transfer Protocol, the networking protocol of the World Wide Web. "http" is also the first four characters of a Web site address (URL).

Icon: A graphical image used to represent an application, file, hard drive, printer, or other object on a computer screen. Double-click an icon to activate it.

Internet: The international, public computer network, composed of thousands of computers networked together. The Internet offers vast sources of information, software, products, and connections to other people.

ISP (Internet service provider): A business that connects individual users to the Internet, usually over a dialup connection. EarthLink is an Internet service provider.

Keyboard shortcut: A command or function initiated by pressing two or more keys at the same time.

Kilobyte: One thousand bytes. Commonly used as a measure of the size of a computer file. Abbreviated as simply "K."

Megabyte: One million bytes. Commonly used as a measure of computer memory capacity in RAM and hard drives. Abbreviated as "MB" or "meg."

Modem: A device that converts computer data into a signal that can be sent over a voice-grade telephone line to another computer. The same device can also decode a signal received over a voice-grade phone line. Your iMac has a built-in 56K modem.

Monitor: A video display screen that provides visual information to a computer user.

Mouse: A device used as part of the interface between human and computer. Movements of the mouse are represented on the computer screen by a pointer, so that a person's hand gestures can be translated to on-screen actions.

ultiple users: A new feature of Mac OS 9 that allows up to 40 different users to create their own personal set of preferences, such as favorite applications, desktop themes, system sounds, and so on. Multiple users are set up by choosing Apple menu⇨Control Panels⇨Multiple Users.

perating system (OS): A collection of computer programs that controls the behavior of a computer, including the manner in which memory and data is organized and stored. The latest Mac OS at the time of writing is version 9.

aste: To insert data stored on the iMac Clipboard into the selected location in a document or application. To paste text you've copied or cut, choose Edit⇨Paste.

ointer: Also known as a *cursor*. The on-screen representation of your mouse. On the desktop, it looks like an arrow. In a word processing document, it looks like the letter *I*.

AM: Random Access Memory. High-speed computer memory utilizing integrated circuits, commonly used for the storage of currently running computer applications and the data files needed by those applications. The contents of RAM are constantly changing and are generally lost if the computer crashes or loses power.

estart: To reload a computer's operating system. To restart, choose Special⇨Restart.

Save: To record the current data or document to the hard drive or other permanent storage media, such as a removable media drive. You should save data frequently to avoid data loss. To save a document, choose File⇨Save.

Scroll bar: A window feature that enables you to view more information than can be displayed in the window at any one time. When scroll bars are visible, you can click the up, down, left, or right arrow buttons, and click-and-drag the scroll box to view information that would otherwise be hidden.

Search engine: An Internet-based program designed to search for information in a database.

Select: The act of clicking an icon or menu item, or highlighting text with a mouse.

Sherlock 2: A new feature of Mac OS 9 used for searching for files on the iMac and for information on the Internet.

Shut Down: A function of the Mac OS that closes all operations of the computer in a systematic manner, so that no information is lost or corrupted. To shut down your iMac, choose Special⇨Shut Down.

Sleep: A function of the Energy Saver feature what shuts down the monitor and spins down the hard drive without completely shutting down the computer. To place your iMac in sleep mode, choose Special⇨Sleep. To reawaken the iMac, press a key on the keyboard.

Surge suppressor: An AC outlet box that includes additional electronic components to protect your equipment from power line surges and spikes.

System Folder: A special folder on the iMac that stores the operating system and other critical applications, utilities, and data files needed by the operating system.

Trash: A special folder that stores files, folders, and aliases intended for deletion. To move a file to the trash, click-and-drag it on top of the Trash icon on your desktop and release the mouse button. To empty the trash, choose Special⇨ Empty Trash.

URL: Universal Resource Locator. The Internet's addressing system. Each document and resource has its own URL, such as `http://www.apple.com` (Apple Computer's home page on the World Wide Web).

USB: Universal Serial Bus. A system for connecting keyboards, mice, and peripheral equipment, including printers, scanners, and removable media drives, to computers. Your iMac has four USB ports, two of which are occupied by your keyboard and your mouse.

Utility: An application that augment or enhances the functioning of a computer or operating system.

Web site: A domain on the World Wide Web. A site is comprised of many Web pages, generally organized around a central theme or topic.

Word processing program: An application for composing, editing, and formatting text documents. AppleWorks contains a word processor.

World Wide Web: A subdivision of the Internet that uses the Hypertext Transfer Protocol to present rich, multimedia content, including text, graphics, animation, video, and sound. Abbreviated as "Web" or "WWW."

Index

Notes